WHY WE KNEEL, HOW WE RISE

WHY WE KNEEL, HOW WE RISE

MICHAEL HOLDING

WITH ED HAWKINS

ILLUSTRATED BY DOUGLAS LOPES

GALLERY KIDS

London New York Amsterdam/Antwerp Sydney/Melbourne Toronto New Delhi

First published in Great Britain in 2026 by Gallery Kids,
an imprint of Simon & Schuster UK Ltd

2 4 6 8 10 9 7 5 3 1

Simon & Schuster UK Ltd
7th Floor, 199 Bishopsgate,
London EC2M 3TY

www.simonandschuster.co.uk
www.simonandschuster.com.au
www.simonandschuster.co.in

Simon & Schuster Australia, Sydney
Simon & Schuster India, New Delhi

The authorised representative in the EEA is Simon & Schuster Netherlands BV, Herculesplein 96, 3584 AA Utrecht, Netherlands. info@simonandschuster.nl

A CIP catalogue record for this book is available from the British Library.

ISBN: 978-1-3985-4290-7
eBook ISBN: 978-1-3985-4292-1
eAudio ISBN: 978-1-3985-4291-4

Typeset in the UK by Sorrel Packham

Printed and Bound in the UK using 100% Renewable Electricity
at CPI Group (UK) Ltd, Croydon, CR0 4YY

FSC www.fsc.org
MIX
Paper | Supporting responsible forestry
FSC® C013604

To all the teachers and
educators around the world
who do a great job

CONTENTS

WHY YOU SHOULD READ THIS BOOK

Knowing lots of things about lots of different parts of life is important. You might be the sort of person who is fascinated by how things work and why. You might be the sort of person who is obsessed with history and how it has shaped the world we live in. You might be interested in science and inventions, sport and incredible adventurers, amazing achievements and stories that have hardly been heard before. You might be interested in impressing your friends with lots of new facts.

If that is the case, then the good news is that this book is for you.

Yes, this is a story about racism and why it exists. But included in this story are all of the things that I have mentioned. That's because the story of racism is the story of life itself. Life in our past, present and future. Knowing about what racism is, why it started and what it means for all of us is important for so many reasons.

I hope this book will help readers become aware that, sadly, there are people in this world who are not treated fairly. And that you will have an opportunity to recognize that and do something about it as you get older.

Maybe you will be inspired to help others. Maybe it will show you the importance of being kind, how to show support to others and how to stand up for what you believe to be right. Maybe it will stay with you for a long time so that the older you get, the more you will be able to spread fairness around your world, among your community and among friends and family.

I hope so.

The book is split into two parts: Why We Kneel, and How We Rise. The first part will explain why racism exists and why there is such anger that it does. It has lots of interesting, sometimes sad, stories about why people have protested against racism by kneeling to show their support. As we go through these stories, I will keep reminding you: this is why we kneel.

It is also a positive book. The second part has stories about how we can rise. How we can improve as human beings, whether white, Black or people of colour, and show all the qualities that I mentioned above: kindness, inclusion and helping others. We can lift each other up! It will even show that it is possible, in time, to stop racism altogether and why that is a good thing for every single one of us.

INTRODUCTION

Hello. My name is Michael. And people used to be frightened of me. I guess I scared people for a job. That's because I was a very, very fast bowler. I played cricket for the West Indies team in the 1970s and 1980s. The greatest sports team ever. Maybe your mum or dad, or their mum or dad, might have heard of them.

Anyway, I bowled so fast that I had a nickname, Whispering Death, given to me by an umpire. It was pretty cool, but only because I had not actually killed anyone. They called me that because the small red cricket ball that we played with is hard and can really hurt if it hits you when someone is bowling it at ninety miles per hour (that's faster than a car on the motorway).

I was very lucky to play pro sports, and between 1975 and 1987, I played 162 matches for West Indies. When I stopped running around cricket fields, I started talking about cricket: I became a commentator. People liked the sound of my voice because I am from Jamaica and have a strong Jamaican accent. That was pretty cool, too.

My life has been pretty good. I have gone about my business quietly. Keeping myself to myself. I played cricket and then talked cricket. That's what people wanted to hear from me. And it suited me because it was easy.

Then it rained.

It was the morning of 8 July 2020 and I was in Southampton. I was supposed to be commentating on live television for Sky Sports as England played West Indies at cricket. But the sky was heavy and dark and full of rain. You can't play cricket in the wet because players slip and slide all over the place and can hurt themselves. Without any action, there was only one thing to talk about: a man called George Floyd.

George Floyd was killed by police in America. A police officer had forced him to the concrete ground and put a knee on his neck. 'I can't breathe,' George said. He said it more than twenty times. George pleaded for his life. He called out for his mum. That knee was on George's neck for nine minutes and twenty-nine seconds. That's a long time (maybe set a stopwatch, or count it on a clock to get an idea).

We know about this because people filmed it on their mobile phones. The videos were seen all around the world and couldn't be ignored. Everybody was talking about racism. The Black Lives Matter movement, which was set up to help stop racism, became very famous. There were protests on the streets in cities all over the world. There were marches. People were asking how and why this was still happening in 2020.

If you were Black, you probably watched the videos and thought: *That could have been me. That could have been a member of my family*. But you also would have known it was not the first time a Black man had been killed by a police officer.

In America in 2020 alone, there were more than 200 shootings of Black people by police. If you are Black, you are six times more likely to be shot by police than if you are white.

It is not just an American problem; let's get that straight early on. There was a man called Christopher Alder who died in a police station in Hull, England in 1998. A video showed Alder lying face down on the floor, with his trousers around his ankles. Police officers were standing around laughing for more than ten minutes (get the stopwatch out again) while Alder couldn't breathe.

Black people suffer. In the US and the UK, Black children are more likely to leave school without having taken exams, we are more likely to go to prison, more likely to live in poverty, more likely to live in poor housing and less likely to own a home. We earn less and, not surprisingly, we don't live as long.

So, given the chance, I thought it was time I said something. And, on live TV, I did. It went something like this:

> *Racism comes from hundreds of years ago. The bad treatment of Black people with slavery is where it started. People will say, 'That's a long time ago, get over it.' No. The world hasn't, so how can the individual?*
>
> *I didn't quite understand as a young man what brainwashing meant – I now understand. People – Black people and white people in particular – have been brainwashed by what we have been taught.*
>
> *Everything should be taught. In my schooldays, I was never taught anything good about Black people, and you cannot have a world that is brought up like that, where you only teach what is easy for*

> *the teacher and what suits a particular story. History is written by the people who do the harm, not by the people who are harmed. By the conqueror, not those who are conquered. We need to go back and teach both sides of history AND TELL THE FULL STORY.*
>
> *Until we do that and educate the entire human race, racism will not stop. We need to teach and re-educate, as a lot of people in this world are growing up believing that they are lesser than or greater than other people, purely based on the colour of their skin, and that cannot be right.*"

At the time, I had no idea if anyone would really listen to what I had to say. But the video went viral. It was watched millions of times and I got tons of positive messages on my phone. I was pleased. I thought: *Great, I have done something – started a conversation. Now I can go away and keep quiet again.*

But a lot of people started asking me, 'What's next?' and saying, 'You can't stop there!'

I got a phone call from Thierry Henry, the great football striker. We had a long chat on the subject, and he said he thought I should keep going.

But I was unsure. I had been running away from facing up to the truth about racism my whole life. I didn't want the attention. In fact, my reply to those who said I should do more was, 'If what I've said on TV isn't enough to explain the situation, then I don't know what else to do.' I even used a cricketing example that I had bowled the ball, hit the edge of the bat and now it was up to someone else to take the catch.

WHY I WROTE THIS BOOK

In the year 2020, I was sixty-six years old, looking back on my life and thinking hard about my choices when confronted with racism. I thought I could have done more.

When I was playing cricket and people from the crowd would say mean or racist things, I should have pointed them out. And talked about it. It would have created a conversation.

As part of a cricket team of mainly Black men who toured the world and had to put up with racism on the field from the crowd, as well as in the towns and cities that we travelled to, I know that as a group, we should have said something. Anything.

It would be easy to argue that I said nothing or the team did nothing because back then, in the 1970s and 1980s, it would have made no difference.

Any sort of complaint might have been seen as moaning. It was a time when racism was everyday. Everywhere. *Sticks and stones will break my bones, but words will never hurt me.* That's what people would say.

The reason I said nothing was because I was totally selfish. When I came across racism, I thought to myself: *These people are sick . . . I'll be going home soon and I won't have to deal with it.* I didn't have to live that life or deal with the daily threat of comments which would make you feel like half a human being. But what about the people who did? I felt like it wasn't my problem. *I'll be on a plane soon*, I would think, selfishly.

At times, the guilt felt heavy. And I have sometimes wondered why I didn't say something. After all, I have had a level of fame which means people are interested in what I have to say, like lots of people who you will read about in this book. My story and their stories are about Black people having their say and telling others what it is like to be treated badly, how it makes you feel and how we can all work together to make it stop.

Maybe I kept quiet because, deep down, I felt that as a Black person, I was supposed to shut up. As you go through these pages, I hope you will begin to understand why it is possible to feel this way.

Maybe it was because I felt that speaking for a few minutes on TV or doing an interview on the radio or for a newspaper was enough.

Maybe it was because I knew that people would get angry. After all, I am not the first person of colour to have spoken up, and I won't be the last to suffer after doing so. If you speak up about racism as a person of colour, you are walking round with a target on your back.

The result of those difficult thoughts is this book. On television, I said people needed to be educated, and that is what this book aims to do. Hopefully, when you have finished reading it, you will be armed with knowledge and facts to help make a difference in the world today, tomorrow and for ever. That's pretty powerful and exciting.

I want to help educate people about why racism exists, how it works and what it is like to be treated differently just because of the colour of your skin. What does it *feel* like when you walk into the room as the only Black person? What does it *feel* like to be looked at like you cannot be trusted? To be followed when you go into a shop? To know that in the eyes of some people, your life is worth less?

An important word to learn in this story is ***dehumanization***.

It's a big word, so we can break it down: *de-human-ization*. This means to not be seen as a human being and to be treated cruelly because of it. The dehumanization of Black people began, and then continued, to make sure that one group of people felt like they were better than another.

To help me tell this story, I have spoken to some of the most famous Black athletes in the world, including:

- Usain Bolt, the fastest man who has ever lived.
- Naomi Osaka, the fierce tennis champion.
- Thierry Henry, one of the greatest footballers of all time.
- Adam Goodes, legendary Aussie rules star.
- Makhaya Ntini, the first Black African to play cricket for South Africa.
- Hope Powell, England's first Black football coach.

I also write about lots of other famous Black sports stars, like Colin Kaepernick, the American NFL player, Lewis Hamilton, the Formula 1 driver, and Marcus Rashford, the footballer, as well as some others you may not be familiar with.

I have also written about Black people who have done incredible and amazing things for the world, but you probably haven't even heard of them. That is linked to what I said earlier about who writes history and who teaches it.

I make two promises to my readers: one – you

will definitely learn something new in this book; and, two – you can use what you learn to help make a difference in the world.

Let's go!

WHY WE KNEEL

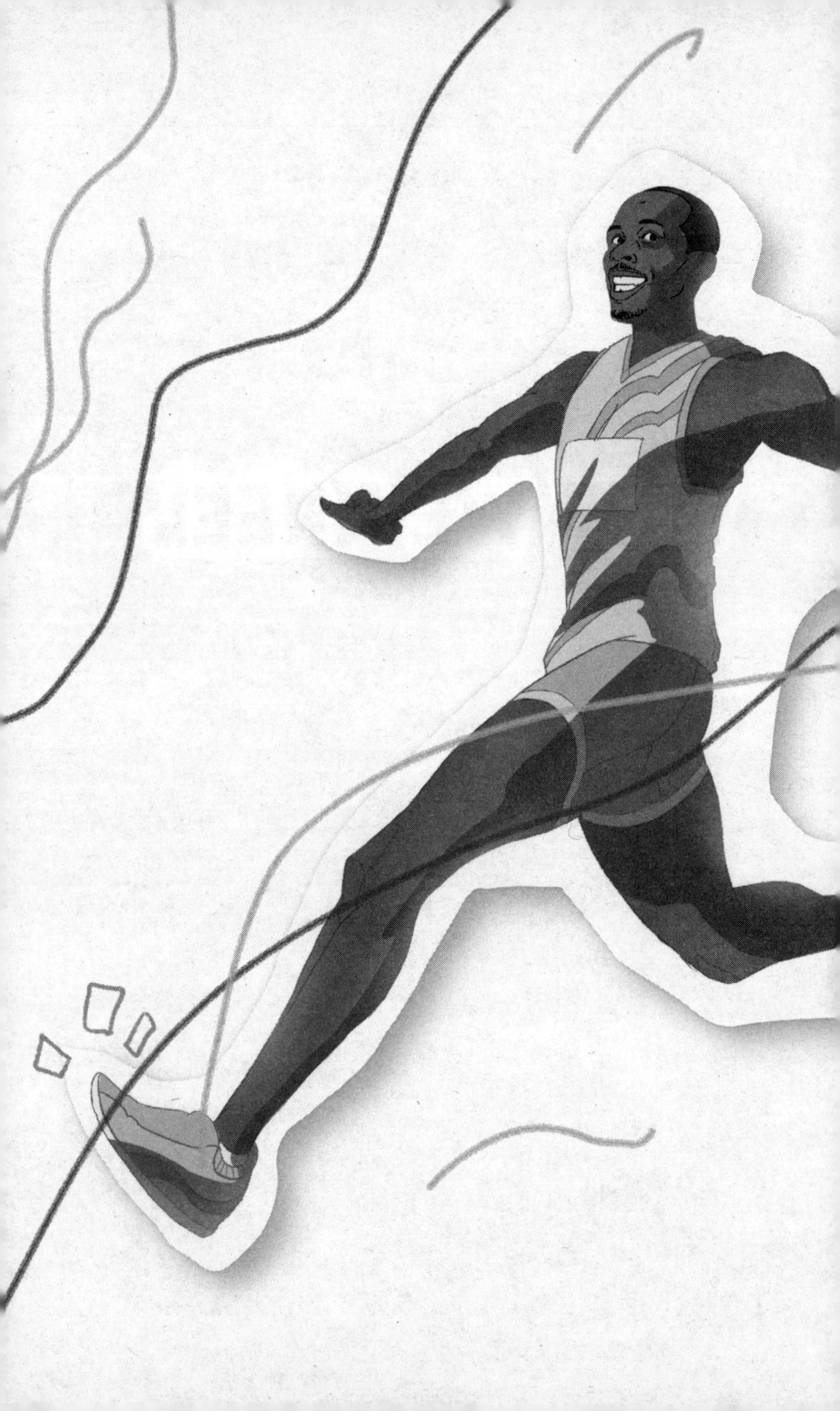

BECAUSE OF RACISM

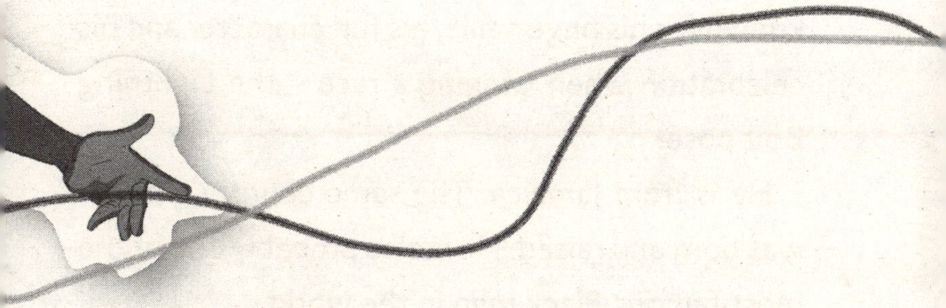

PROFILE: USAIN BOLT

Usain Bolt is the fastest man in the world. The greatest sprinter ever. He is a history maker. Usain set the world record for the fastest 100 metres in 2009, running it in just 9.58 seconds. That means he can run the length of a football field in ten seconds. His top speed was about 28 miles per hour. Next time you're in a car, keep an eye on the speedometer and you will get an idea of how quick that is. Wow.

Usain also broke the world record for the 200 metres, running it in 19.19 seconds. He won eight gold medals in three Olympic Games. He was also known for his huge smile, his fun character and his celebration when winning a race – the Lightning Bolt pose.

He is from Jamaica. The same country where I was born and raised. He is also probably one of the most famous Black men in the world.

When I spoke to him for this book, he told me an interesting story.

When he was around twenty years old, making a name for himself as a professional athlete, he was in London for an athletics meet. He had some time off, so thought he'd do some shopping. He walked into a shopping centre. After a while, he noticed a security guard was following him around. *Strange*, he thought, but continued shopping. He went into a jewellery store because he was interested in buying a watch.

He told me what happened next: 'I said to the woman behind the counter, "I like this one . . . How much?" And she says, "Are you sure you can afford it?" I was thinking, *Why is she thinking I can't afford the watch?*'

'That wouldn't happen now,' he then said. Well, he's right about that.

When I was a young man, the exact same thing happened to me. I asked to see a watch and, before the lady took it out of the display cabinet, she told me the price in a voice which suggested I could not afford it. It was as if she wanted to save herself the effort. I noticed the attitude immediately and just said, 'I'll take it,' before she even took it out, just to shock her. It was more money than I'd wanted to spend, but there was no way I was going to give her the pleasure of saying in her mind, *I knew it*.

In Usain's case, it is a ridiculous and shocking story because he is instantly recognizable in every corner of the globe. Everywhere he goes, people know who he is: the fastest man in history. The greatest. And yet, back then, he was made to feel like he was nothing.

'I just remember thinking, *Could you show me the watch?* I didn't understand,' he told me. 'And I didn't think back then, *This is racist*, because it was new to me. As an experience, it was unpleasant, but good comes from telling it.'

Usain remembers that story – and I remember mine – because of the way it made us feel. It hurt then, and it still does now. That's because we were both made out to be lesser humans. Remember that word: *dehumanization*? There are a lot of stories like that in this book. They are not coincidences.

I wanted to ask him about growing up in Jamaica. What was his upbringing like? What were his views of racism at the time? What was he taught at school? But I quickly noticed he was very keen to make his voice heard about race and racism because he has so rarely been asked about it.

'It hurts to see it. My heart bleeds to see the [bad things] still happening. In this day and age, why would it still exist?'

As we know, Usain is one of the finest athletes of all time. His fame, his strength, his speed and his character make him stand out. He is proud of his Blackness. And Black people are proud of him. As a man who is often seen as superhuman, he is an example of what Black people can do if they are just given the chance. But does it also mean he is 'protected' from the everyday racism that others experience?

'I'm not sure "protected" is right,' he says when I ask the question. 'Okay, I don't get followed by security guards any more. You might not be in a situation to be abused on the streets or to be kneeled on or choked. But you see it around you and, as a Black man, you'd be, like, "Whoa, those things are still happening today." It's affecting you like anybody else. The things that you're seeing of late, nobody's thinking, *Oh, I'm protected*.'

But we were protected in a way: we had grown up in Jamaica, a country where there was very little racism by the time we came along. Jamaica was, and is, a largely Black country. It wasn't always that way, of course.

When Jamaica first became a British colony, meaning it was owned by the British Empire, around 80 per cent of the people who lived there were white. By the time Jamaica was freed of British rule in 1962, the population was 0.7 per cent white.

'We grew up in a rural area; we didn't know racism,' he explains. 'You didn't know that thing existed. It was very community-based, very loving. We were just kids having fun, playing cricket, playing football. We just would not have experienced it.'

Snap. Usain and I had the same upbringing, even though we grew up years apart. We were the sort of boys to be outside all day: kicking a football around, playing marbles, riding bikes or making a ball out of tape and string to play Catchy Shubby – a type of cricket which always seemed crazy because there were so many people taking part. We used an old bin for the 'stumps'; Usain used to carve them into a tree. Matches would last hours. Our mums would be calling us to come in for supper as the sun went down. And the kids we were playing with? They almost all looked the same as me. But the few who didn't, we didn't notice. We were just kids having fun.

In school, there was no education around racism, apart from information about what happened during the slave trade. If you wanted to find out, you had to educate yourself.

Usain tells me that when he was in high school, he started to take an interest in what was actually happening outside of the Caribbean, in places like America and the UK. When he wasn't running, playing football or playing cricket, he would talk with friends about Black history.

'We spent a lot of time discussing great achievements in Africa,' Usain says. 'And people don't know that Africa used to be a major centre for worldwide trade before slavery destroyed that. And the great mathematical and scientific achievements of Africa. There's plenty to show Black pride in.'

There was no real education about racism at home either, or about what was happening to Black people elsewhere in the world. I am sure I never even heard my mother use the word *racism*. Family life was instead all about being polite, looking smart and working hard.

Usain agrees. 'Yeah, those sorts of negative things or feelings . . . we wouldn't have dwelled on them. My parents wanted me to be happy and positive. Maybe they thought if they had talked about such things, it could have made me worried about the future. I'm not an athlete who is angry and trying to say, "You were wrong." God blessed me with a talent and I tried to make the best out of it.'

What Usain and I have in common, you see, is that we had to leave Jamaica to be educated about racism. In our home, we felt safe. But when we left, we were told 'you don't belong'. And that only changed when we became famous for doing well at sports. That doesn't seem fair or right, does it? Usain, when he tried to buy that watch, wasn't accepted. He is now. He had to become the fastest man in the world to be accepted. This is a very important point. Just to be treated like an ordinary human being, Usain had to do something extraordinary. Black people often have to be famous or well known to be treated in a fair way. This is a good example of what racism is. But let's look at it more closely.

I guess before we learn more about racism and why it happens, it might not be a bad idea to start by learning exactly what it is. We can break it down pretty simply.

Racism is when one person treats another person badly or in a negative and different way because they have a different colour of skin.

So, when a shop assistant assumes that Usain Bolt can't afford a watch because of the colour of his skin, she is treating him in a negative and different way to how she would treat a white person. This is racism.

If I apply for a job and am not given it because I have Black skin, that is racism. The same if I'm told I can't eat in a certain restaurant or sit in a certain train carriage. It is racism if a person of colour is not given the same chance to do something that others have.

If I am shouted at and called names, is it racist? Well, not necessarily. BUT, if that person talks about the colour of my skin, it is racism. Because the colour of my skin should not matter.

Let's think of an example. Say I knock over someone's drink in a cafe. They get angry and shout, 'You idiot!' Not very nice, but not racist. If they shout, 'You Black idiot!' then they are being racist, and that is more hurtful because the fact I am Black shouldn't come into it.

What I'm trying to say here is that the colour of your skin should not matter. It should not stop you from buying a watch. Getting a job. Eating in a restaurant. Anything. I think we can all agree that we want to live in a world where anybody can get the chance to achieve anything they want, and there should be nothing to stop them doing that.

Sadly, we don't live in that world. If you have black or brown skin, it is very, very likely that you have suffered in some way or been treated differently. I am hoping that people like you, reading this now, will be able to do something about it in the future. To use the words in this book as inspiration to fight for the right of people of colour to be treated as equal.

So why does racism exist? Well, the short answer is that it was a way to make sure that one group of people got the most chances to achieve anything they wanted. Racism against Black people has been going on for hundreds of years, and to understand why, we need to understand the HUGE part that slavery has played.

BECAUSE OF SLAVERY

You've probably been taught about the African slave trade at school. It was a deeply dark and disturbing time in history, the fallout from which we still feel today. But it is worth revisiting some important facts and dates related to this as they will help explain the central points that come up throughout this book.

First off, the African slave trade was also known as the transatlantic slave trade because slaves were taken across the Atlantic ocean. It started in the 1500s and lasted about four hundred years, and it mostly involved European countries forcibly taking people from their homes in Africa and shipping them to the Caribbean and America. Around 12–15 million Africans were forced into slavery, and when you add in the number of people who did not survive the awful conditions and the journey across the sea, you can imagine that it actually involved way more people in total.

Those who arrived to their destination worked long hours, for no money, on what were known as plantations, harvesting crops like sugar, tobacco and cotton. These goods were then taken to European countries to be sold, making lots of people (and countries) extremely wealthy. The British Empire, France, Spain and Portugal were the largest slave-trade participants.

As I said, you've probably already been taught this. But maybe you haven't been told how it was allowed to happen.

HOW DID SLAVERY HAPPEN?

When I was growing up, my dad was a strong, quiet man. He didn't talk much, but when he did, everyone listened. I remember going to work with him one day. He was a builder and ran construction sites. He was the same there – quiet but firm. If something was wrong or someone did something bad, everyone knew it because he would speak up. I've become a lot like my dad. If someone treats me unfairly, I'll say something. But otherwise, I'm fine staying quiet.

I am like this because of something called *learned behaviour*. We all learn a lot from our parents and guardians, or the people around us. Babies start learning as soon as they're born – for example, copying the faces they see from very early on. As they grow up, they keep copying: how to talk, how to sit, how to react to things. We even learn how to show our feelings, like raising our voices when cross or hugging someone when we want to show affection. Much of who we are comes from watching and learning from others, especially our loved ones.

If you think carefully about it now, what things do you think you might have picked up from those around you? Do you have the same look on your face when you are trying to work out an answer to a question? Do you like the same food? Do you laugh at the same things? If you answer yes, then that is quite possibly because of learned behaviour.

Learned behaviour isn't always good. Sometimes it's like brainwashing, where we believe things just because we've been told them over and over again. *Brainwashing* is a scary term, but it is hard not to use it when we are talking about what has happened to Black people throughout history. For example, my mum's family didn't want her to marry my dad because his skin was darker than hers. Can you believe that? I am the youngest in my family and didn't know about it for years because they didn't talk about it, pretending it wasn't a problem. But that silence was a form of learned behaviour, too.

This happens not just in families, but in wider society. *Society* is a collection of people living together. It's your village, town, city, country. The world, even. Now, society teaches us how to behave. In good ways and bad. We learn what to do and how to talk on television or through the internet.

Some behaviours have been handed down from governments to the people, teachers to pupils, parents to children, like a nasty habit, for hundreds of years. When people are told something over and over again, when they see it and when they hear it, it becomes as natural as the spring moving on to summer. *That's the way it's always been*, like a tradition or a recipe. Or, *Well, we always do it like that*. Have you heard these types of sayings?

For many years, it was taught that Black people were not as good as others. This idea was planted in people's minds, and it grew over time. This led to terrible things, including slavery. It wasn't just one person waking up one day and deciding to enslave others.

BECAUSE OF PAYING THE TRADERS

HOW DID SLAVERY END?

The British Empire decided that it should stop its involvement in the slave trade in 1807. The United States did not ban it until 1865.

So, all over, then. Done and dusted. Nothing more to worry about. The trade in Black people was over and slavery was finished. Black people could, finally, live a life of freedom and be given the same chances in life as their former masters, right? If only it were that simple. Unfortunately, changing laws does not change the attitudes and thoughts that have been formed over centuries.

In America, Black people were not truly free anyway. The American Constitution, which is basically a rule book for how the United States is run, was written in a way that meant white people could say that Blacks were not as important.

We can also see that the terrible treatment of Black people and the deep-rooted belief that they were inferior would continue in the fine detail of how slavery ended. So, let's think back to all those millions of Africans who were forced onto ships, the millions who died and the millions more who were treated badly. With slavery ending, surely African people were going to be given an apology or help to try to recover, right? Wrong.

Slavery ended because the people who made vast sums of money from it – the traders in sugar, tobacco and cotton – were told: sorry about ending slavery, but here's a load more money to make up for it.

In short, the traders had to be paid off with vast sums of money to stop stealing human beings. This was called *reparations*. For the misery they inflicted, they were paid. I will say it again. The slave owners were paid. Not the slaves. The British bill in today's money was estimated at about £100 billion. No one seems to be sure of the exact sums but the French government were said to have demanded around 100 million gold francs (about £14.7 billion today) in 1825 from the country of Haiti, where they had sent many slaves to work for them. The bill the French made them pay for their freedom was ten times the country's annual revenue and was only paid off in 1947.

Britain's bill was not paid off until 2015. That basically means, all people paying taxes in the UK were helping to pay off the former slave owners who were being compensated for their 'loss'. That means that if your mum or dad, or grandparents, were working at their jobs up until 2015, they would have been paying money to the former slave owners. And that includes Black people, too. I feel like I am going to write this a lot in this book: does that seem fair or right to you?

In America, compensation was rejected by slave owners in the South of the country. The people who argued against slavery and those who argued for it would clash in a bloody civil war. The

American North wanted to end slavery. The South wanted to keep it.

DID YOU KNOW?

There were people in the American South who were trying to help slaves. One of the most famous was Harriet Tubman, who was born into slavery in 1822. She helped other slaves escape thanks to something called the Underground Railroad. It was a maze of secret routes and houses – run by those who believed slavery was wrong – where Black people could be kept safe.

It was Harriet who helped slaves find their way to the Railroad and taught them how to use it. She had escaped, herself, in 1849. This was a very dangerous thing to do, and if caught, she would have probably been killed. Despite the danger, she completed about thirteen missions, helping around seventy people escape.

WHAT HAPPENED IN AMERICA AFTER SLAVERY?

Although slavery was illegal in America by 1865, attitudes did not change overnight. A slave didn't go to bed on Monday and wake up a free man, with all the benefits of a white person, on Tuesday. That was impossible. Slavery continued, just in a different form.

America needed these free workers to make its money. The American South had lost the Civil War to the North and was now flat broke. So the Black man couldn't simply walk out of the plantation on that Tuesday morning to a new life. No way. The 'former' slave owners in the South and the lawmakers needed to come up with a new way to make sure he was not liberated.

A NEW SLAVERY

Although the transatlantic slave trade had been banned, people were still traded inside the country. The number of slaves would nearly triple in the next fifty years, so that by 1860, there were almost 4 million slaves in America.

Laws were introduced to make it illegal for a former slave to be without work. But how would a slave, who would often be illiterate (because it was illegal to teach a slave how to read and write) and have skills only suited to slave work, get a job? To add further obstacles to freedom, if a Black man was found on the street, he could be arrested and beaten. So they stayed on the plantations.

Those who stayed, called *sharecroppers*, had to earn their freedom, and those who didn't suffered a worse fate, which we will get to later.

Sharecropping was when the masters gave the slaves the tools and the seeds to plant the crops. These were given in the form of money. Harvest a certain amount of crops, and your money – or debt – is paid. Of course, the slave owners made sure the terms of this deal were ridiculously unfair to the slave and his or her family. Rarely was the debt ever paid off.

There were other discriminatory laws designed

to target formerly enslaved people, too, including Pig Laws. Where if, for example, somebody stole a pig worth, say, $1, they would go to jail for five years. Strangely, a lot of Black people, yet barely any white people, were convicted of such crimes. Black people were also arrested for looking at white women, being homeless and, well, just sort of wandering around with nothing to do, otherwise known as 'loitering'. The punishment was up to twelve years in prison. And, as you can imagine, with the 'freed slaves' unable to get jobs, there was a lot of wandering around with nothing to do.

So, basically, if you didn't stay on the plantation, you were almost certain to be arrested. You had a choice: stay as a slave or go to jail. So, the number of Black people in prison grew and grew. Black people were an impossible position.

FROM PLANTATION TO PRISON

So, what to do with all these Black prisoners? thought the people in power in the American South. *Put them to work!* It's almost as if they had planned to convict Blacks for made-up crimes so they could get free labour again. If you're thinking, *That was exactly their plan!* I think you're right.

This was called *convict leasing*. From courthouses and jails, men were sent to local plantations or factories. And by 1894, around three-quarters of the money made in Alabama, one of the largest states in the South of America, came from this practice.

Convict leasing was not much different to slavery. Businessmen paid money to the prison, which meant they sort of owned the prisoner, agreeing a contract that they would be put to work. The prisoner would only be free again once the cost of his purchase had been paid off through work. But guess what? Strangely, a lot of the time the agreements made were 'lost', so the prisoner could never pay the money back and was never free.

Peonage was another horrible way to continue slavery in the South. The US Constitution (remember, that's the 'rule book' by which America is run) said that slavery was illegal, but that there was a way to get around it, which read: '*except as a punishment for crime*'. The old slave owners would pay to prevent a Black man from going to jail for one of the many made-up crimes mentioned earlier. And that man would then work, for free, until the debt was paid off. And guess what? Oh, I'm sure you've probably worked it out by now . . .

So much, then, for the end of slavery. And so much for the end of Black people being dehumanized. This is an important point, because history books will record the end of slavery by the British and Americans, and everyone will think: *Phew! Glad that's over . . . It ended a long time ago – why are Black people still going on about it?* We are still 'going on about it' because the truth is never taught. And dehumanization has not stopped. Blacks were treated as less than human before slavery. They were treated as less than human during slavery. They were treated as less than human after slavery. And the story continues . . .

MORE VIOLENCE

Sadly, in America, the bad treatment of Black people would never really stop. Despite slavery being made illegal, things just seemed to get worse and worse. Violence against Black people was normal, and it wasn't only by slave owners. Whole towns and communities just let it happen.

It is a very unpleasant part of history again, but we shouldn't be afraid of reading about horrible moments in the past because I think it helps explain the present and can help us shape the future.

Between 1877 and 1950, there were at least 4,384 lynchings in America. What is a *lynching*? Well, a lynching is an illegal killing, usually carried out by a mob. Most of the time the victim is accused of a made-up crime, and after slavery became illegal, Black people became the primary targets of white

Southerners in this horrible act of violence.

Most of the lynchings happened in the South of America, but they occurred all over the country. Why? We know why, of course. Because Black people were not seen as human. And, with the so-called 'freedom' of Black slaves, white people felt their own way of life was being threatened.

Going to watch a lynching was considered a day out, like a family outing to a cricket or football match. Mums, dads and children. Thousands and thousands would turn up to watch a Black person be murdered. It is unbelievable, but it really happened! Postcards of the event were sometimes sold. The only 'crime' these Black people had committed was to have Black skin. You may be wondering what the police were doing. Were they allowing this to happen? An event called the Tulsa Race Massacre helps explain.

THE TULSA RACE MASSACRE

On 31 May 1921, Dick Rowland, a Black nineteen-year-old whose job was to clean shoes, was arrested in the city of Tulsa in the state of Oklahoma in the South of America. A white woman had said that he'd assaulted her, but this was a lie. The fake charges were dropped, but police kept him in jail to protect him from an angry white mob that had gathered outside the station to lynch him. A large number of Black people came to the prison to help protect him, too.

Reports from the time show that the white mob were given guns and bullets by other policemen, who began to shoot at the Black men protecting Mr Rowland, forcing them to retreat to Greenwood, a neighbourhood famous for being a strong and successful Black business district. The white mob, including police, followed and started shooting at any Black person they saw, burning homes and buildings as they went. Survivors reported that planes from a nearby airfield also dropped firebombs on Greenwood.

More than 10,000 Black people had to leave their homes and up to 300 Black people were killed but no one can be sure because, surprise, surprise, no proper records were kept. No members of the white mob were punished.

The attacks were designed to make sure that white people remained at the top of society, and Black people at the bottom. No excuse was in fact needed for the violence. And that's the way the mob wanted it: to frighten Black people into thinking that if they made any mistakes, they could be killed. Things like:

- Accidentally bumping into a white person in a shop
- Speaking in a supposedly rude way
- Refusing to step off the pavement when a white person came by
- Using the wrong title for a white person.

The lynch mobs were encouraged by racist leaders,

politicians and authorities of the day. US President Woodrow Wilson had refused to support an anti-lynching law despite at least one happening every week.

BECAUSE OF FAKE SCIENCE AND INFLUENCERS

Human beings often think that people different from them are not as good, and this idea helps create racism. Racist ideology has been spread through books, religion and even fake science.

Hundreds of years ago, as Europeans looked to be the leading force in the world, some of these ideas were used to help them.

Let's think about religion for a minute. If you have ever been in a Christian church in Europe, you may have noticed a picture or painting of Jesus Christ. What was the colour of his skin in those pictures or paintings? I bet that he had white skin. He may well have had blue eyes and blond hair, too.

Now, if we think really hard about where Jesus was born, or where he was from, how likely do you think it was that he had white skin, blue eyes and blond hair? Jesus was from a part of the world now called the Middle East, which back then stretched from north-east Africa to India, where almost everybody had brown or dark skin. Jesus was a brown-skinned Middle Eastern man. But he is never shown like that in Europe. Why?

Jesus is used as an example of goodness and purity, so many people think this is to show that European people, or people with white skin, were better than people of colour.

There was a study done at a famous American university called Stanford in 2020. Children were asked to draw a picture of what God might look like. They had all colours available to them. Most of them drew a God who was white.

This is an example of false imagery. Maybe they did that because they have learned, or believe, that being white is best. Fake science is another important part of racist brainwashing. There are lots of examples of so-called scientists making things up to falsely 'prove' that white people were better than anyone else. Some of them are so silly, they are almost funny. Let's look at a few.

CAROLUS LINNAEUS, EIGHTEENTH-CENTURY SWEDISH BOTANIST, PHYSICIAN AND ZOOLOGIST

In 1735, Carolus Linnaeus put human beings into four categories based on where they were from: America, Asia, Africa or Europe. And he gave each of them a type of character. Americans were bad tempered and stubborn. Asians were sad and greedy. Africans were lazy, untrustworthy, careless and unreliable. Europeans? Well, wouldn't you just know that they were calm, strong, gentle, clever and inventive.

PETRUS CAMPER, EIGHTEENTH-CENTURY DUTCH PROFESSOR

Petrus Camper's idea to make Europeans think they were the best really wasn't very clever at all. He used Greek statues to rank the beauty of human faces. He did this by drawing a line from the forehead to the jaw and another from the ear to the base of the nose. The faces were then rated into groups; apes, average faces, beautiful faces and classical statutes. That a lot of Black people were put in the ape group helped racism to rise.

SAMUEL GEORGE MORTON
MID-1800S AMERICAN SCIENTIST

Samuel George Morton was the guy who reckoned intelligence was linked to brain size. After measuring a vast number of skulls from around the world, he concluded that white people had larger skulls than other races and were therefore 'superior'.

All of this is considered gibberish now, of course, but it was considered science back then. And you can't argue with science, right? With such supposedly intelligent people having their ideas published, and everyday citizens taking them as fact, we had a situation where racism became normalized. Instead of racism being something that had been invented by humanity to justify its worst side, it had suddenly become something which was presented as a scientific fact, like gravity. So, from a very long time ago, these ideas were put into people's heads, and we've been trying to get them out ever since.

GREAT THINKERS?

It wasn't just religion or 'science' promoting racist ideas. Some of the world's most famous great thinkers (or philosophers) were also doing it.

Immanuel Kant, who is pretty famous for being brainy, said in 1781: 'The race of Negroes can be educated, but only as slaves . . . The Americans [here he was referring to the original, very first Americans, who were not white] cannot be educated, they care about nothing and are lazy.'

François-Marie Arouet was a philosopher who

was also known as Voltaire. He remains very famous to this day and is also classed as very brainy. He said all creatures should be graded and that Black people were at the bottom, just above monkeys. Remember what we said about dehumanization? You see, people were being told that Black people were not human; they were like animals. He even wrote that Africans were 'animals' with a 'flat black nose with little or no intelligence'!

It is important to understand that these people were admired and listened to. They can be compared to the Instagram influencers of today or those who have lots of followers on other social media platforms. People looked up to them. They believed what they said. They were being educated to think, *It's okay to treat Black people badly*.

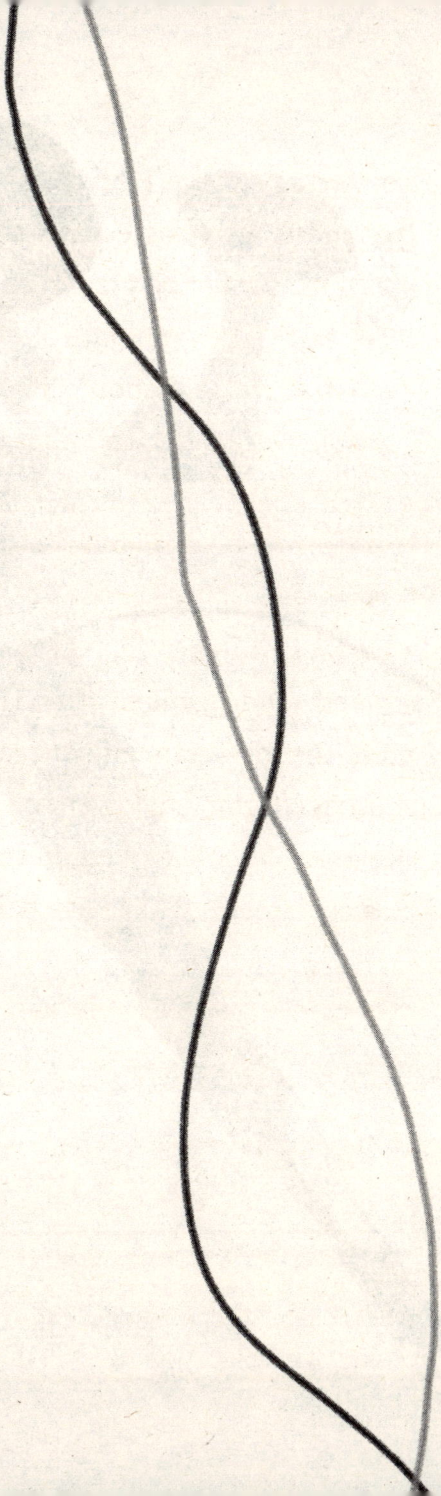

PROFILE: COLIN KAEPERNICK

Colin Kaepernick's story is one of the most incredible in this book. You may not believe it when you read it, but it is all true.

The easiest place to start is at the beginning. Colin was a professional American football player. He earned millions of dollars playing for the San Francisco 49ers. He was a huge star, and he played in one of the most important positions in the team: quarterback. There have been very, very few Black quarterbacks in the history of American football. In the 2012-13 season, he almost led them to win the Super Bowl, which is the most important competition in the sport.

By the end of the 2016 season, however, his career was over. He would never play again. Why? Because he stood up for Black people. Or rather, he sat down.

Colin was sick and tired of Black people being killed by the police in America. And in 2016, after three Black people had been shot and killed by police, he said *enough*. In a pre-season match, Colin decided he would stay seated when the national anthem was played. Normally, all the players and the coaches have to stand up when it is played. Colin didn't budge. A reporter noticed he was sat down while his teammates stood around him.

Colin said, 'I am not going to stand up to show pride in a flag for a country that oppresses Black people and people of colour. To me, this is bigger than football, and it would be selfish on my part to look the other way. There are bodies in the street and people getting . . . away with murder.'

In the fourth pre-season match, Colin did not stand again. Instead, he knelt down on one knee. This was the start of a worldwide protest in sports where athletes would, as I'm sure you've heard, 'take the knee' in protest against racism. Colin took a knee in every game that season. His teammates and coach supported him. The title of this book *Why We Kneel, How We Rise* comes from Colin's protest. Hopefully you are beginning to learn 'why we kneel'. Later, we will get to the 'how we rise' part, which will show how the whole world can get up off their knee and stand tall and proud after doing the right thing by treating people fairly.

Anyway, you can guess that lots of people in America were angry. Colin left the San Francisco 49ers team at the end of the season and no other team in the league would take him. Everyone in the sport knew that Colin was a great player and should have been part of a team. But lots of people believed that the owners of the teams had got together and agreed not to sign him because they didn't want to upset their fans. Almost all of the team owners were white, by the way, and Donald Trump said NFL owners should sack players who took a knee.

Colin kept speaking out and did lots of charity work. He gave more than one million dollars to charities and set up a project called Know Your Rights, a group which educated young people about the law. It was hoped that this would help Black people know what to do if the police were causing them problems.

In 2018, Nike used Colin in an advert which said, 'Believe in something. Even if it means sacrificing everything.'

Colin's story meant a lot to me. And it made me think deeply about my own life as a professional sportsperson. When I was playing, I could have spoken up, could have stood up when I saw and heard racism. I should have; I know that. But I did nothing. I was not as brave as Colin.

But you know what? All the anger that Colin caused and the fact that this ended his career meant that the story wouldn't go away. The Black Lives Matter movement and protests and marches got stronger and louder because of those types of reactions. It just showed that Colin and people like him were right.

Black Lives Matter. Taking a knee. Everybody knows those phrases now.

Black Lives Matter (BLM). When I say those three words, I am saying that Black lives have mattered less for hundreds and hundreds of years, and it's time something was done about it. Over the course of this book, I want to show exactly why something has to be done about the treatment of Black people. I'm not saying that Black people matter more than white people, or any other race, and it is frustrating when people say that is what the BLM movement is about. Maybe if we just put the word *too* on the end, people wouldn't complain. Black Lives Matter, too.

'Oh,' some say, '*all* lives matter.' If only that were true. It is so obvious that all lives do not matter because it is Black people who risk death when leaving their front door in America, Black people who are followed by shop security, Black people who are mistreated and Black people who are judged just because of the colour of their skin.

White privilege is another term you might have heard. This is very difficult for some people to understand, and it makes some people very angry. Because *privilege* is a word that some think is related to money or material things. 'I'm not privileged,' they might say. 'I can barely put food on the table.' But it is not meant to describe how much money you do or don't earn or what luxury items you have. It's not about the size of the house you live in or the number of cars you drive. The privilege is . . . not having to put up with everyday racism.

That word *privilege* in 'white privilege' relates to the fact that there are fewer roadblocks to doing well in life if you are white. If you are a white school kid going into a corner shop to buy some sweets, it is unlikely that the shopkeeper is thinking you are going to steal something. If you're a Black school kid doing the same, history tells us that the shopkeeper might not be so sure. The privilege here is that the white kid isn't looked at with as much suspicion.

I have an Irish friend who once said to me, 'Mikey, I know what it's like – we have had a rough time as well.' I had to disagree a bit. The Irish have been treated badly in history, but no one knows you're Irish until you open your mouth. For us Black folks, everyone knows we're Black from a hundred metres away, and we are judged on sight. He understood.

BECAUSE BLACK PEOPLE WERE NOT SEEN AS HUMAN

By the end of the nineteenth century, with Europeans dominating the world, it was obvious that the people from those countries who were powerful believed, absolutely, that they were better than other people, in every sense. Just because of the colour of their skin. As we have discussed, those who were not white were considered in-human. They also had no rights and were treated like they had no physical or emotional feelings, no hopes, no dreams. They were cargo.

This is dehumanization again. Without it, slavery could not have started, survived and succeeded.

The way Black people were transported on ships from one side of the Atlantic to the other is the most obvious example of how Europeans thought Black people were less than human.

They treated animals better.

There was no space on these boats. People had to lie tightly squashed together, often on top of one another. They had no room to move. They couldn't stand or sit. They had to go to the toilet there, too. Imagine that. No, you probably can't. Horrible.

There was no fresh air or sunlight for weeks. As you can imagine, the smell was pretty bad.

Sickness was high and people got ill very quickly. There was almost no food or water, and anything that was given to them was old and dirty.

These conditions were extremely harsh and cruel, and many people didn't survive the journey. The horrors of slavery are clear for all of us to see now. But when they were actually happening in real time at the height of the trade, there were few prepared to protest.

DID YOU KNOW?

The slave ship Zong departed Africa in September 1781 with 470 slaves on board – more than it could actually hold, by the way, but many captains overloaded their human cargo to make as much money as possible.

When the Zong got stuck mid-Atlantic in a part of the sea called the doldrums, *where little or no wind could leave ships stranded, the crew and slaves began to die of illness. The captain threw more than 130 slaves overboard. Were people angry at this mass murder? Not really.*

Criminal charges against the company, the captain and the crew were dropped. Britain's solicitor general said of the case, 'What is this claim that human people have been thrown overboard? This is a case of goods. Blacks are goods and property; it is madness to accuse these well-serving honourable men of murder. The case is the same as if wood had been thrown overboard.'

IN-HUMAN

If slaves were 'lucky' enough to survive the journey across the Atlantic, things improved very little once they arrived. They would be greeted by men like Edward Long, a British-Jamaican slave owner, who said his money-making plantation was okay because Black people were not only inferior but not human. 'An orangutan husband would not disgrace a negro woman,' he wrote. This meant that he thought that Black people were like orangutans.

Such views meant that barbaric conditions for slaves on Caribbean plantations were not given a second thought. If a slave was not sold at auction, they were often just left to die. The cheapest slaves were bought with the idea of working until they could no longer work. Families were separated. Usually they were branded with their master's initials. To be branded was to have your skin burned by a boiling-hot piece of metal so people would know who owned you.

The working hours were from dawn until dusk. At harvest time, it meant eighteen hours in the fields. Punishments like having iron chains hung around the neck or being physically harmed were normal, even for small mistakes like letting a pot boil over.

In the American South, Black people's status as in-human was made law. In Virginia, it was written that it was not a crime to kill a slave. This was known as the Casual Killing Act, a law needed because of the sheer number of slaves dying as a result of owners punishing slaves for small things. The law basically said that it was the fault of the slave for doing something wrong, like running away.

Why were such laws needed? Well, it wasn't just to make it clear that slaves were seen as in-human. It also acted as some sort of protection for the slave owners, in case any of these people felt some guilt for what they had done. They would be able to say, 'I was just trying to teach them a lesson . . . The law says that's okay.' The key words in the lawbook that protected slave owners for beating Blacks to death were 'should chance to die'. So you were covered if you beat them to death by accident. How hard is it to beat someone to death by accident, do you think?

MEDICAL EXPERIMENTS

At a time when Black people were not considered human, it was normal to use them for medical experiments. Operations on Black slaves happened without any form of pain relief because it was believed that they felt less pain than white people. Often these operations took place because doctors and surgeons were trying to find the best way to treat white people. Once they had figured out how to do them, the operations, with pain relief, were made available to white people.

One of the people who carried out these operations was called James Marion Sims. Some of his most gruesome experiments were on Black babies. What he did is far too upsetting to write here, but it is worth noting that Sims was so famous and celebrated that there were statues of him in America. One was still on display in New York as recently as 2018. That's a pretty upsetting thing for Black people to see, knowing what he had done, don't you think?

Some say that Black people should 'get over' slavery because it was a long time ago. But its impact has touched every single one of us. And that, as I said earlier, is learned behaviour. Black people still suffer the mental scars of that time. The idea that they are worth less, that they are bottom of the pile and should just be grateful that they now have their freedom has been passed down through the generations. Slavery was a horrific, brutal and chilling part of making sure Black people were treated as though they were worth less, but it was just the opening part of the story.

BECAUSE OF SEGREGATION

In the American South, there was also something known as *segregation.* Segregation means the separation of people into racial or other ethnic groups. For Black people, this translated into not having the same rights or access to the same spaces as white people. The laws of segregation were known as Jim Crow laws. Jim Crow was not a person. He was a stage character played by a white man with his face painted black. The character, who was dressed in rags, would sing and dance and was shown to be lazy, stupid and worthless. *Jim Crow* was used as an insult. Hence its use in the name for laws that made Blacks second-class citizens. The Jim Crow laws were in place from the 'ending' of slavery until 1965. Most historians recognize that it was just slavery by another name. Guys, I was born in 1954. It's not that long ago.

The laws were different city to city, but here's a list of things Black people could not do:

- Go to a whites-only school
- Get on a whites-only bus
- Eat in restaurants
- Go to see a movie
- Own a home
- Own a business
- Freely move from city to city, town to town.

Black people were also often denied the right to vote if they failed 'literacy tests'. These were supposed to be easy reading or writing tests, but they were designed to make sure no one passed. Can you answer any of the questions that were used:

- How many bubbles are in a bar of soap?
- How many windows are in City Hall?
- How many seeds are in a watermelon?

How did you do? Not so well, I'd guess.

Eventually, segregation on the grounds of race, religion or where you were from was banned, and not giving people jobs because of these things was made illegal. A very important Black man called Martin Luther King had a lot to do with that. These reading and writing tests were banned in 1965, and in 1968 laws were also passed allowing Black people to own or rent a home. I know it seems like a long time ago, but there are people alive today who remember this time and it's an important piece of the story, reminding us why we learn about history, what really happened and why we kneel.

DID YOU KNOW?

Who was Martin Luther King? Well, he was one of the most important people in Black history. Without him, Black Americans would not have had any rights at all. He was known as the leader of what was called the Civil Rights Movement in the 1960s. This movement was fighting for Black people to be treated fairly, equal to everyone else. He gave a very famous speech called 'I Have a Dream', where he demanded an end to racism in the USA. One of the most famous parts read: 'I have a dream that my four little children will one day live in a nation where they will not be judged by the colour of their skin but by the content of their character.' It was pretty cool.

Without Martin Luther King, America would not have laws which make racism illegal, Black people wouldn't be able to vote and there wouldn't have been laws to help them to live in better homes. And I guess you could say that he is a reason for us to all rise. Of course the American government tried to stop him. He was threatened, spied on and labelled as the most hated man in America. He won the Nobel Peace Prize in 1964. Four years later, he was shot dead, aged thirty-nine.

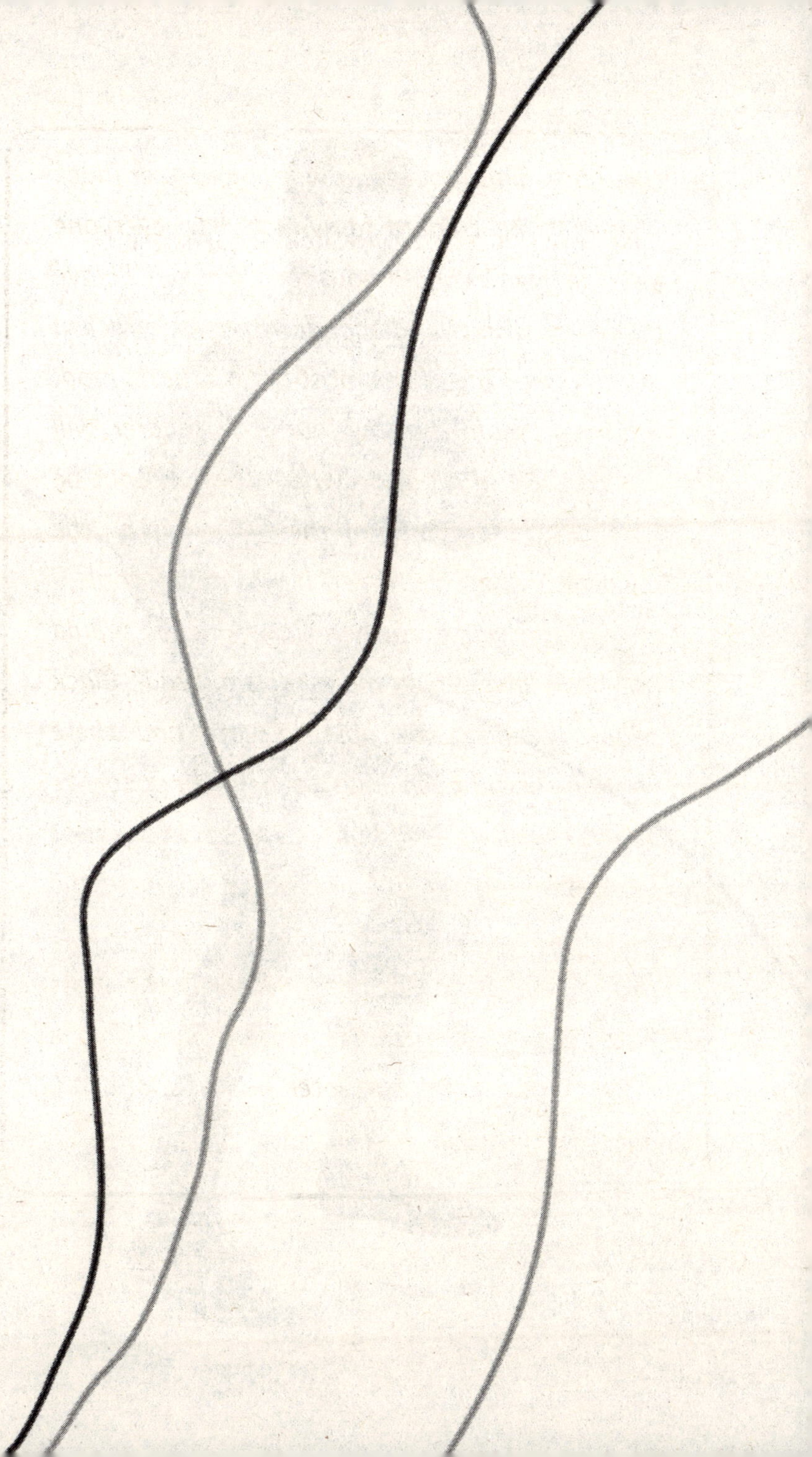

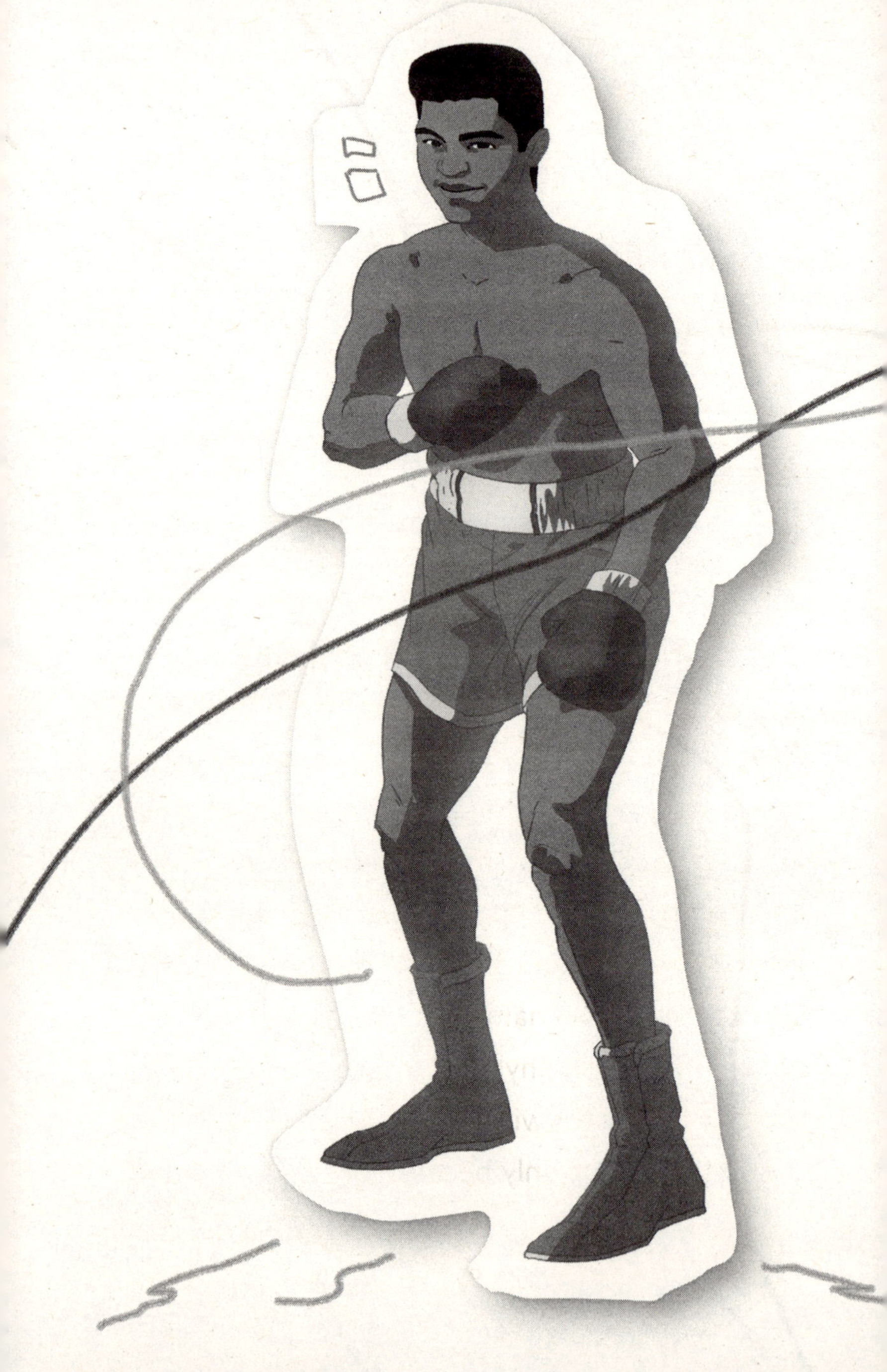

PROFILE: MUHAMMAD ALI

A lot of time when you hear people talking about sports stars, they might say 'he or she's one of the greatest'. Those two small words – *one of* – are important. That's because the real, undoubted greatest was a man called Muhammad Ali. It has become like a nickname for him. Nine times out of ten, if you ask anybody to name the greatest sportsperson, they will say his name.

And that is not only because of what Ali did as

a boxer, but also as a human being to show that Black people were not treated fairly.

Ali was born in 1942 in Louisville, Kentucky in the USA. Or rather, I should say, Cassius Clay was born there. Ali would later change his name as he became more aware of how it affected him. He became a Muslim and decided that Cassius Clay was a 'slave name'. He said, 'Why should I keep my white slave master's name visible, and my Black ancestors invisible, unknown, unhonored?'

He came from a family who had been slaves and grew up in a time when there was racial segregation. His mother told a story that when he was a boy, he went into a shop to ask for a glass of water, but they refused because he was Black. She said it really affected him. Worse was to come. When a boy called Emmett Till, who was fourteen, was murdered and lynched by white people for supposedly offending a white woman who ran a shop, Ali later said, 'Nothing would ever shake me up (more) than the story of Emmett Till.'

After his bike was stolen, Ali, then twelve, took

up boxing in case he needed to defend himself or his belongings. He trained hard and would end up having one hundred fights as an amateur, losing only five, and winning lots of championships, including a gold medal at the 1960 Olympics in Rome. It is said that he threw that medal into a river after he was not allowed to eat in a whites-only restaurant.

In 1960, Ali turned professional, and he quickly set about beating everyone. He became the heavyweight champion of the world when he toppled the fearsome Sonny Liston in 1964. The way Ali danced around his opponents in the ring and the speed with which he threw punches made him a very exciting boxer to watch. He beat Liston again in a rematch in 1965. Ali was on his way to legendary status, and not just because of his boxing skills.

America was fighting a war in Vietnam, and in 1967, Ali was told to join the army. This was the law. He refused. His reasoning was simple: 'Why should they ask me to put on a uniform and go ten thousand miles from home and drop bombs and bullets on brown people in Vietnam while so-called Negro people in Louisville are treated like dogs and denied simple human rights?' Ali was arrested. He was fined $10,000, which is almost as much as $100,000 in today's money, and sentenced to five years in prison. He never actually went to jail, though, because straight away he appealed against the judge's decision.

Unsurprisingly, Ali was banned from boxing and was no longer world champion. He received death threats and was spied on by the US government. Instead of boxing matches, he toured the country speaking against the war and in favour of Martin Luther King's Civil Rights Movement. 'Black men would go over there and fight, but when they came home, they couldn't even be served a hamburger,' he said. People were listening to Ali. They realized that he had given up everything for the cause: his career, his money, his freedom.

In 1970, aged twenty-eight, Ali was allowed to box again. He won his first two fights, which put him in line for a shot at the world title against Joe Frazier, but Ali lost for the first time in his professional career. They fought again in 1974. Ali won this time.

Ali's most famous fight was against George Foreman, also in 1974. It was called 'The Rumble in the Jungle' because it was held in Kinshasa, Zaire, in Africa. No one thought Ali had a chance at winning because he was getting old. To everyone's amazement, Ali won the fight and became world champion again. One billion people watched on television around the world, a record at the time.

But as I said, Ali wasn't just one of the best boxers ever. He was a poet, a singer (a lot of people thought he helped to invent rap music), actor and TV star. His work helping Black people continued long after he stopped boxing. He donated millions to charity, toured the world to speak about racism, helped people realize that in some African countries, people were dying because of drought and famine, and visited loads of countries at war to try to stop the fighting. All of these things show that Ali was by far the Greatest.

PROFILE: IBTIHAJ MUHAMMAD

There are people who have the power to force change. Ibtihaj Muhammad is one. African-American. Muslim. A woman. Those are some pretty big hurdles to clear right there. She was born 4 December 1985 and early on in her life, she decided she was not going to apologize for who she was. She wanted to beat the system that put up barriers, obstructing the hopes and dreams of so many like her. And then smash them down.

She did it. Even though she experienced shocking moments of hate, 'Those spurred me on,' she told me. 'To keep [me] focused on the mission.'

Ibtihaj won a bronze medal in fencing for America in the 2016 Olympics in Rio. She'd only started competing at the age of seventeen and had won five Fencing World Championship medals, including gold. She is the first ever US Olympian to compete while wearing the hijab, a head covering worn in public by some Muslim women.

After her Rio success, she was named in *Time* magazine's '100 Most Influential People'. *Time* is a pretty big deal. It is one of the biggest and most famous magazines in the world. In February of the same year, she was invited to a private meeting with President Barack Obama alongside other famous Muslim Americans. He looked for her in the audience. 'Where's my Olympian?' he said. 'Stand up,' he added, urging her to take the applause.

That sure is something. But America is a country where you can be picked out by the president one day and be accused of being a terrorist another. That happened to Ibtihaj when walking through Times Square in New York. A man – she managed to take a photo and put it on social media – followed her for several blocks and started shouting at her. No one around her did anything to help. Although I grew up in Jamaica, protected from racism, Ibtihaj experienced it from the word go.

Ibtihaj is important because she beat the system which was built to stop her. She grew up in New Jersey in a town called Maplewood. Her dad is a retired police detective; her mum a teacher. She went to Duke University and studied International Relations and African-American Studies, and Arabic. She was already outstanding before she competed for her country. How did she do it? Well, she had parents who rallied against the system.

'I was blessed with a mom who is an educator,' she says. 'She was always challenging us. And she held our teachers accountable; there was no getting one over on my mom's kids. And I always wonder what happens to those kids who have working parents who don't have the time to put in or they don't know that maybe their teacher does not have your child's best interests at heart.'

When she was younger and her parents warned her that life might become difficult as she made her way in the world, she remembers saying to them, 'Nah, white people aren't like that.' Ibtihaj learned the hard way.

She suffered years of racist behaviour from staff and some teammates as a fencer. Her name was left off official team sheets, she was excluded from team emails and not invited to team dinners. She reported this to USA Fencing, the organization who runs the sport in her country. Nothing was done.

So, what can we do to change it?

'The answer is education,' she says. 'Black history is not really taught anywhere. Unless you think it started with slavery.'

BECAUSE OF HOW WE ARE TAUGHT IN SCHOOL

The way slavery is taught in schools is a good example of how racism is whitewashed (which means lots of the horrific detail is skipped over), making it easier for racism to live on today. *Africans were stolen from their homes and put on ships; lots of them died; the ones who didn't were treated badly and made to work all day for no money; and then this thing called slavery was stopped. The end.* It is not taught in a way that shows why racism still exists, that shows why we make that protest, why we kneel.

I was taught about slavery at school, and I don't think I enjoyed my history lessons very much. Learning about it, as a Black person, made me feel like a lesser human. And by that, I mean I felt that somebody, somewhere was saying to me, 'Hey, this is where you came from, so don't get any ideas that you can *be* somebody.' My ancestors were brought over in chains from West Africa, so I should be grateful that people like me had 'progressed' and that those days were gone. There was very little focus on the brutality of the slave trade.

I obviously didn't have that specific experience in Jamaica, but don't forget that when I was at school (all those years ago!), we were an island which was owned by Britain. And Britain chose what was taught and how it was taught. And you can't blame the British for that. Anyone else would have done the same. The British role in the slave trade – and how much money they made – was not taught to me at school. Nor to my sister, Rheima, who is twelve years older than me; or to Marjorie, my other sister, who is ten years older than me.

So could, perhaps, another story be told about Black people which is not just about how we were seen as poorer, weaker and less clever people?

Guess what? Black people had a story before

slavery. Below are three things which are not often taught:

SEPTIMIUS SEVERUS

Julius Caesar is the name most people remember when they hear about the Roman Empire. He came, he saw, he conquered. But not many know about Septimius, an African emperor from 193 to 211. Yes, you read that right. There was a Black Roman emperor. He was also one of the most important, ruling the empire at its peak, when it covered more than 5 million square kilometres. He was born in Libya, Africa, in 145 AD and died in York, England, in 11 AD.

THE MOORS

Black people brought such change and great ideas to the world. They were called 'the Moors'. *Moor* was a another word for African. William Shakespeare, the most famous writer that ever lived, used it to describe Black people. But the word has also been used to describe Muslims in Spain and Europeans of African descent from 711 to 1492.

In 711, a group of North African Moors captured a place called Al-Andalus, which is known today as Spain and Portugal, which meant historic change in Europe. The Moors' knowledge in mathematics, astronomy, art and farming helped Europe out of the Dark Ages.

The Moors represent just one African group of people. There are loads that we don't learn about. Why, for example, are we not taught about the trade routes to Asia from West Africa? Or the amazing building works in Zimbabwe thousands of years ago?

THE REVOLUTION IN HAITI

This was pretty amazing. Enslaved Africans overcame French colonial rule in Haiti when they said *enough*. The slaves went to war with their owners in a fight for freedom, outnumbering them ten to one. It started in 1791 and was led by a Haiti-born former slave called Toussaint Louverture. Three years later, the French government were forced to free all slaves and make them full citizens. Haiti, the independent nation, was born in 1804.

DID YOU KNOW?

Rebecca Lee Crumpler was the first Black woman in the USA to qualify as a doctor. She had her own medical clinic in her home in Boston and treated people even if they couldn't afford to pay. Then there was Bass Reeves. He was one of the first Black US Deputy Marshals. He was born a slave in 1838 and is said to be the man who the Lone Ranger was based on.

DID YOU KNOW?

Katherine Johnson was an amazing person. Not only did she have to overcome being treated differently as a Black person, but also as a woman. She worked for NASA, where a lot of men made all the decisions. She was like a human calculator. She was a genius at maths. It was her job to work out the best time to launch crewed space flights, the routes they should take, and the path they should take if they needed to return in an emergency. Without her, NASA would not have been successful in the first ever crewed space flights and loads more after it.

BECAUSE OF THE BRITISH EMPIRE

I played cricket for West Indies. And we beat everybody. But did you know that the West Indies isn't actually a country that exists? It's a collection of islands and small countries which get together so they can have the best and strongest cricket team.

The British Empire was sort of like that. It was like a team of countries that were all connected to Britain, providing it with things to use, sell and make money from, all to make Britain the best and strongest.

In the fifteenth century, the British decided that they wanted to start exploring the world. They went to North America, Africa, Asia and the Pacific. They went to countries there and, basically, took over. They took land and resources for their own gain. The local people had to work for Britain. This is called *colonization*.

It doesn't seem fair to me. But there are some people who don't agree. In 2016, a survey was done in Britain and it found that as many as four in ten people thought that the British Empire was 'a good thing' and colonialism was something to be 'proud of'. Only one in five British people thought that the Empire was something to regret. Do you think that might be because of what they were taught about in school?

The true history of the British Empire is simply not taught. And you can hardly blame the British because, honestly, it was not a nice thing. They invaded. They used violence to get their own way. They took away the local people's freedom. And they stole. The British are largely unaware of what really happened. Here are just three things which might show the Empire in a different light:

THE BENGAL FAMINE

Bengal was a place in India under British rule. In 1943, a lot of crops – which provided food – failed. So what did the British do? They took more and more of the healthy crops, like rice, to feed those who were fighting in the Second World War. This meant that prices for food in Bengal went up because there was much less available. The result was the death of 3 million people in Bengal. In total during the British rule of India, tens of millions of Indians died of starvation.

THE BOER WAR

Ever heard about the Boer War? I doubt it, because it's not often taught in schools. This was a war fought over diamonds and gold in what is now South Africa. The British wanted all of that good stuff for themselves. But so did the Boers who had lived there and believed the diamonds and gold belonged to them. The British won and set up prison camps in which they kept up to 150,000 Boers in terrible conditions. Around 30,000 of them died, including women and children.

THE BERLIN CONFERENCE

During the Berlin Conference of 1884, all the powerful European colonial nations – including Britain – got together to have a chat about how best to make as much money as possible from their colonial project. It's worth remembering what 'colonial' means here. Simply, it means that one country takes over another to control its resources and benefit from them. At the conference, countries were divided up between colonial powers. It was reported in newspapers in Africa like this: 'The world had, perhaps, never witnessed a robbery on so large a scale.'

GREAT BRITAIN?

People in Britain aren't really taught about the bad things that happen to create an empire. If they were, do you think more might believe it was something to regret? Or that it was wrong? I do. And as I said, I don't blame Britain for not wanting to teach the bad stuff. They are probably embarrassed, so they try to keep it quiet. There is a popular meme that sums this up well: on one side is a picture of a cuddly dog with the caption, *The Brits in British history books*, and on the other, a snarling, dangerous-looking dog with the words, *The Brits in every other history book.*

It is true that Britain had a big role in ending slavery. They did so in 1834, thirty-one years before America. But forty-two years after Denmark. William Wilberforce, the politician who was leader of the group to end slavery, took about twenty years to convince the British parliament that slavery should be illegal. In that time, hundreds of thousands more slaves were taken by British ships. Wilberforce is a name that is taught in Britain's schools. The motivation to end slavery was something called *reparations*. This was the payment scheme which rewarded slave owners and demanded slaves work for another four years to earn their freedom. In 1834, Britain spent 40 per cent of its budget (taxpayers' money) on compensating slave traders.

And this is probably a big reason why the truth about slavery and the British Empire is not taught. It creates knowledge, which leads to anger, which leads to protest for things to be put right. But isn't anger greater when you find out that you have been lied to? Isn't it easier to forgive when someone has said sorry? The British government has never formally apologized for its role in the slave trade. It is my belief that they think that if they started teaching this stuff properly, they'd have to start paying for it. Perhaps they think: if it isn't taught, people will forget.

HOW ARE THE OLD SLAVE COLONIES DOING?

Cities like Glasgow, Bristol and Liverpool were rich in the eighteenth century because of slavery. Meanwhile, the Caribbean was poor and playing catch-up on educating its people. After colonization, 60 per cent of the islands' Black population couldn't read or write. Disease and poor health was everywhere because for hundreds of years, people were brought up on a sugar-based diet. That was what the plantations produced, so that's what those who worked there were fed. We are still feeling the effects of that today, with the Caribbean people having one of the highest rates of heart problems in the world, while Barbados and Jamaica are listed as 'amputation capitals of the world' because of the prevalence of a disease called diabetes. Shouldn't there be true 'reparations' for that?

How does it make a Black British person feel when they do their own learning about what really happened? They might feel that their country has lied or hidden things from them, doesn't value them or their culture, doesn't see them as part of the fabric of the nation and, worst of all, has fed the racist abuse that has impacted their lives.

A fair and equal society would teach a fair and equal history. But we know society is neither of those things. So a fair and equal history of Black people is not taught. It is not because Black history started when they put the first set of chains on a Black person and took them from one place to another. That is the history that has been chosen to suit the story.

PROFILE: HOPE POWELL

After the end of the Second World War, Britain was really poor. It had no money because fighting a war is very, very expensive. Britain also didn't have many workers. The war could be blamed for that, too, because of the large number of people who were killed and wounded by German bombs or while fighting.

Between 1945 and 1946, the number of British people able to work fell by more than one million.

Some were moving to places like Australia, New Zealand and Canada. The British government's answer to this problem was to invite people from the Caribbean, including my island, Jamaica, to come to live and work in Britain. So people from the Caribbean came. We took work in factories, helped run public transport, worked in the NHS. They needed us, so we came.

There was a famous ship called *Empire Windrush*, which arrived at Tilbury docks in 1948 carrying 492 West Indians keen to start a new life. They were the first of many. Between 1948 and 1952, some 1,000–2,000 people entered Britain each year, and by 1956 there were around 40,000 West Indian immigrants in Britain. One of those who came was a lady called Linever Francis. She arrived in England on 25 November 1963, married and raised two children, a son and daughter. Her daughter was called Hope.

Hope Powell's story provides hope for the future. She was the first ever Black coach of an English national sporting team when she took on the role of England women's football manager in 1998. She was the coach of Brighton and Hove Albion Women. Then she took a job at Birmingham City FC. She has done brilliantly despite racism being a real problem in England's national sport. She has inspired people of all ages, races and backgrounds. Hope is the living example of what Black people bring to a country. And she is the perfect answer to those racists who say, 'Why don't you go back to where you came from?'

Twelve years younger than me, Hope grew up on an estate in Greenwich in south London. When I was in England for the first time in 1976 playing cricket against England, she was aged just ten, learning about racism, just as I was.

'I have this vivid, grim memory of being a child,' she told me. 'This old white woman shouted to me as I was walking past her, "Why don't you go back to where you came from?" I didn't understand what she was talking about. After all, I was born in England. This country was built on immigrants. And then you want people to go back? Why don't they know this?'

Hope knows why people act this way. I know too.

It is because they were never told why people from the Caribbean came. Not by the government. Not by television or newspapers. Not by schools. In fact, a survey was done in 1955 which said that two-thirds of British people had a 'low opinion of Black people'. Remember what we have learned so far about habits being passed down the line from parent to child?

Like so many people of colour, Hope and her family bore the brunt of this ignorance.

'My mum and brother were in a park, and there was another child there, a white kid. My brother was reaching out to him. The mother of the white child hit my brother to get him away from her child,' Hope recalls.

As well as this abuse, Hope's mum had dog poo put through the front door.

So, we know about learned behaviour. But what were people being taught when Hope was growing up? Let's have a mini history lesson. Here are some important things that happened between the 1960s and the 1980s:

- An MP called Enoch Powell made a famous speech in 1968, now known as the Rivers of Blood speech. It was an anti-immigration speech that used lots of racist language. It stirred up hatred towards people of colour. And when an MP says such things, it gives everyday folk the courage to behave badly. That is as true now as it was then.
- Then the government – which, don't forget, *asked* Black people to come and help – started making laws. One was called the British Nationality Act (1981). It was written to say who and who could not live in Britain. It felt like people of colour were now not wanted.
- In 1993, a Jamaican lady called Joy Gardner was killed by police who were trying to arrest her to send her back to Jamaica because of these new laws. It was like the George Floyd murder before camera phones.
- The police had a group called the Special Patrol Group, which seemed to drive

around London looking for Black people to bother from 1961 to 1987. They targeted Black people under another new law, which allowed police to arrest anyone they thought was ABOUT to commit a crime. Strangely, a lot of Black people found themselves in cuffs for just standing about.

- There were riots in Brixton, London, in 1985 when police shot Cherry Groce because they thought she was *going to* commit a crime. Cherry was unarmed and had been shot 'by mistake'. She was paralysed for life. The police officer who shot her was not punished. It took the police twenty-nine years to apologize.

In 1985, Hope was nineteen. Had her mother told her about racism as she grew from a girl to a young woman?

'She did,' Hope says. 'But I'm not sure that I understood it. And I guess, growing up, I think I was aware of the differences. I think I tried to, and still do, live in hope that people just accept it.'

Hope said her mother told her the only way out was education. Her mother also made sure that every time they went out as a family, they looked really, really smart, to try and make sure people wouldn't pick on them.

When Hope started playing football, the racism was often not as bad as in everyday life. She was called names on the pitch and in the stands, but she was always supported by her teammates.

Hope played sixty-six times for England as a midfielder, scoring thirty-five goals. Her first game for England came when she was just sixteen and she played in the 1995 Women's World Cup. Three years later, she was made manager of the national team, leading them to the World Cup quarter-finals in 2007 and 2011, and the European Championship final in 2009. She also reorganized the coaching of the women's game from Under-15 to Under-23 level, and she was the first woman to achieve the highest coaching qualification possible. Some people say that the Lionesses would not have won the European Championships in 2022 and in 2025 without her laying such strong foundations.

Hope recalls, 'One thing I was absolutely clear in my own mind [was] *I cannot fail*, and I knew people would say, "Look, we gave a Black person a chance; we gave a female a chance, and they couldn't do it." That was in my head constantly. And that is the case still today.'

Hope has come a long way. But has Britain? A study found that 18 per cent of the British public thought some races or ethnic groups were less clever, and an amazing 44 per cent thought some groups of people were more hard-working than others. That's really sad. And Hope is just one example of how wrong those people are.

COLUMBUS THE LIAR

We can't blame just Britain for ignoring parts of history. The whole world has been doing it. And there is no better example than the story we are told about Christopher Columbus, the supposed daring and exciting explorer. Columbus was Italian, and in the 1490s, he set out on his ship to discover new lands for his employer, the Spanish royal family. He was aiming for Asia, but actually ended up in what we now know as the Americas. He was the man who discovered America. Wow! He found it? Can you imagine? No. Me neither. Maybe that's because it wasn't true. Did you know, in fact, that most of what we have been told about him is a lie?

For a start, when Columbus arrived on the shores of the Bahamas, which is in the Caribbean, he wrote in his diary that there were people living there. They were called the Arawaks. So how can he have 'discovered' America when there were people already there? The answer is that he did not discover it. He just told Spain and the rest of Europe that it was there. We don't go on holiday somewhere for the first time and come back and say we discovered somewhere completely new, do we?

Columbus, though, is remembered as some sort of hero. But he is another example of a person being celebrated for killing people who had different colour skin. He called the Arawaks stupid and said he wanted to make them slaves. And he did exactly that. He beat and killed them.

Columbus continued sailing around the world 'discovering' other countries, too. It was the start of *colonization* (another word for building an empire) and slavery. The exact number of people who died because of Columbus is not known, but it has been estimated to be many millions because of the rise in violence and disease left by his 'adventures'.

THE FIRST EXPLORERS

There is loads of evidence that African explorers were in America hundreds of years before Columbus. African presence in the 'New World' (land and countries that the Europeans had newly discovered) has been said to date as far back as prehistoric times, 40,000–6,000 BC. People from a place we now call Egypt arrived in the Americas around 1200 BC, while the Mandinka people from

West Africa arrived about 1307 AD.

We know this because of Columbus's diaries. He wrote that Native Americans had traded in gold-tipped metal spears with black-skinned people. These spears were found to be exactly the same as those found in West Africa. Lots of experts have shown that there were Africans in America and Mexico before Columbus.

BECAUSE OF WHO IS TEACHING YOU

I think we still need to ask these questions: How are you taught? And who by? It is a very difficult job to try to change what is learned, but it is nothing compared to the mammoth task of changing people's actual minds and teaching them in a different way. And by *different*, I mean the stories and histories of Black, brown, white or any other colour people, all being treated and taught in the same way.

In an effort to show you how big a problem this is and has been, we need to go back in time again.

This time we're off to Britain in the 1960s and 1970s. Black kids would suffer racism in their everyday life, but you'd probably expect that school was something of a safe place. Unfortunately, it wasn't.

In the 1970s in Britain, the Black child was treated as someone who wasn't really worth teaching. The words used at the time were *educationally subnormal* or ESN for short. So Black children were sent to ESN schools. Loads and loads of children were taken out of the normal school system and placed into these schools.

Why? For the simple reason that they were different. As you have read, after the Second World War, Britain needed help from the West Indies because Britain was poor and didn't have enough people to do the jobs that needed doing. So lots of families from the West Indies answered that call for help and came to live and work in Britain.

For some reason, it came as a surprise to the people in charge of education that the children of those coming might find it difficult to adjust to a completely different way of life. Schools didn't want those kids, with many saying, 'If the Black kids do well here, more Black kids will come . . . and we don't want that.' So Black kids were put in ESNs.

What was an ESN school like? Well, if you were sent to one, you were almost certain to work a low-paid job after leaving. Children barely received an education there.

BERNARD ON THE CASE

The person who spoke out about the ESN schools was a writer from the Caribbean called Bernard Coard. He had been a teacher in ESN schools. He wrote a book about what he saw and how Black children in Britain were not being educated properly. He explained that these children were just as clever and keen as anybody else. What do you think happened to him as a result?

To start with, he was called a liar.

Then, it got worse. Bernard's phone was bugged so that the authorities could listen to his conversations. He and his wife were followed by people working for the government and his nephew was harassed by police.

Luckily, lots of people – including from the

newspapers, TV and radio – did listen to Bernard. Six months after publication, education authorities admitted his book was 100 per cent accurate. ESN schools were eventually closed down.

If you were a Black child at school in Britain in the 1960s and 1970s, and you did well, you did so without the help of the education system. Bernard's book meant that Black families and friends decided to set up their own schools, which opened on weekends. There were more than 150 of them. Some of them taught the real Black history.

Sadly, the impact of ESN schools is still being felt today in Britain. All those children who were let down, not taught properly and treated badly would have really struggled to get good jobs. I'm sure your mum and dad are often telling you how important it is to get a good education so you can get a decent job. Well, most ESN kids didn't stand a chance. And those kids are now grandparents or parents who have probably struggled to put food on the table. If you grow up poor because a parent has been unable to get a good job, you are more likely to suffer in the same way. It is like a chain reaction, and it keeps happening. We need to break the chain.

AND WHO ARE YOU TAUGHT BY?

It is not just about *what* you are taught, though. It is also *who* you are taught by. And just like the rest of us, teachers are part of a world that says racism is okay.

In my life, teachers are thought of as really important people. Four members of my family are teachers. My mother taught for more than fifty years and eventually became a headteacher; my eldest sister taught; my younger sister's daughter taught; and my eldest daughter teaches, too. So it's important I make this clear: I am not blaming only teachers or saying they are the BIG problem. I just want to explain how they – and you and me, and everybody else – are part of the problem.

Sadly, the racism people suffer starts as soon as they enter the classroom. A 2016 study carried out by the US Department of Education – interviewing more than 50 million students – found that Black students in America are nearly four times more likely to be suspended as white students and nearly twice as likely to be expelled. Black pre-schoolers (that's an age range of two and a half to five) are 3.6 times more likely to be suspended. At the time, Black girls represented 20 per cent of the total number of girls at pre-school but made up more than half of pre-school child suspensions.

We don't even have equality in the classroom at that young age, so it is hard not to worry about this and think, *What chance do Black folks have in life?* But teachers can, and probably will, go a long way towards solving this problem because they are brilliant.

JEFF AND PHILIP: A STORY

One teacher, Jeff Harriott, is trying to help. Jeff is originally from Australia but moved to Britain and is now headteacher at a school in Manchester. He sent me an email after he saw what I said on TV about how people need to be taught about why and how racism exists. This what he wrote:

> “*I guess it's a bit like trying to open a locked door and no one will give you the keys. We can bang and bang, but ultimately we have two choices: we can walk away, it's too hard or we knock the thing over and open up new possibilities. What is taught at school is always changing and what you have said is making sure that we are even clearer on what we need to do. Your voice, your comments, you will have an everlasting impact on our school.*”

And I guess Jeff's words helped me to find the

confidence to go ahead and write this book. I hope some of these pages will be useful to help students learn.

I spoke with Jeff to find out more about how education can be made better. He told me a story about his early days in teaching. He was teaching a class that had a Black boy, who we will call Philip, whose mum was from Zimbabwe, Africa. Teachers had struggled to control the class, but when Jeff turned up 'all was good'. After all, he was from Australia. Philip loved his accent. He would talk to him about *Neighbours*, the TV soap opera, and kangaroos. But then the relationship started to break down. Philip ended up hitting Jeff, who had criticized the boy for bad behaviour and not listening. But Jeff later realized Philip's mum was working long hours at home, they had escaped from Zimbabwe because of the dangerous situation in the country and that Philip was basically very unhappy. Jeff learned that he had failed to do his job.

Jeff says, 'I had no understanding of what it

was like to be him. It wasn't that his behaviour wasn't his fault, but it was me who was to blame for not making school a place for him to behave in the right way. This is what I think happens too much in teaching, and particularly towards Black boys. Teachers don't understand what the boy is going through. One of the big problems is that not enough people try to walk in somebody else's shoes.'

A MOTTO

'Take a walk in somebody else's shoes.' That is a good motto for life. It means you are imagining about what it is like to be someone else. I believe we have done that so far in this book. Thinking about being someone else doesn't always mean you are dreaming about being Lionel Messi or Cristiano Ronaldo or a famous movie star. It means, for example, you think about what it is like to be someone from a different country, or with different colour skin, or from a different religion.

When you have read the stories, the history and things that have happened to others, have you thought, *What if that had happened to me? How would I have felt? What would I have done?*

Schools could ask and answer questions like, What does being seen as different mean to those people? What does that mean for their lives? Not just, 'We're going to have an Eid party, an assembly and then go home for tea.'

This gets to the very heart of the problem, because if we have teachers who are struggling to understand people of a different colour, culture or religion, we risk making people feel like they are outsiders. And a child who doesn't feel a part of something is going to find school hard. Sports stars are a great way of making people feel both represented and inspired. And that is one of the ideas behind this book. I am trying to say, look, you can be like this person.

PROFILE: MARCUS RASHFORD

British people love football. But they also like to make fun of their footballers, or say that they are stupid or selfish. Maybe it is because they are jealous of all the money that they earn.

Marcus Rashford is a superstar footballer who is very hard not to respect. He is another Black sportsperson who has noticed that he can use his fame for change. He has probably achieved more off the pitch than on it, and for that, some people still criticize him. But you can't please everybody.

Marcus's family are from the West Indies, and his early life was hard. His mother didn't have much money and she would skip meals to make sure he and his four siblings had enough to eat. But football would become a way out.

Marcus has already done more in the sport than most can dream of. He has played for Manchester United, one of the biggest clubs in the world, having joined at the age of just seven. He scored two goals on his debut, which was in a European game. And then he scored in his league debut against Arsenal three days later. He had a habit of scoring on his debut. He did so again when he played his first match for England in May 2016, becoming the youngest English player to score in his first international. He has played in two European Championships, the first in 2016 when he was the tournament's youngest player.

Marcus also has an MBE. But he didn't really get that for his football.

In 2019, his life changed. Marcus set up a campaign

with Selfridges called In the Box to help homeless people over Christmas. He and his mum would visit shelters to help hand out packages of food and other things the homeless needed. They also sent packages to children's homes in the Caribbean.

During the COVID-19 lockdown, Marcus realized that lots of families and young children were struggling. They couldn't get to the food banks or places which helped them because no one was allowed to go outside. A lot of poor children, for example, were not getting their free school meals because the schools were closed! He started to work with a charity to help feed them. At the start, the aim was to help 400,0000 children in and around Manchester. But it was so successful that more than £20 million was raised. Children all over the country were now getting help.

Matt Hancock, the MP who was in charge of health during the pandemic, had criticized footballers for earning too much money and not helping the country. Marcus made him look very silly, particularly as he started protesting about the government's plan to take away free school meals for poor children in the summer holidays, gaining a lot of attention in the press. The government had no choice but to do what Marcus wanted and keep the meals.

Marcus then started the Child Poverty Taskforce with food shops, manufacturers and delivery companies. While this was happening, Marcus had a petition to pressure the government to give more money to help stop child poverty. The government couldn't ignore him for long and said they would give £400 million over twelve months to support poor families with food and bills.

And Marcus kept going. He put pressure on the government to provide more money for poor people, started a campaign to help people learn how to cook cheaply and helped with a project to get young people reading. He even wrote a book called *You Are a Champion*, which won an award.

EQUAL?

One of my earliest memories is from when I was six years old. I climbed into bed one December night with my mum and dad. They were listening to the radio reports from the 1960/61 West Indies cricket tour of Australia. I remember snuggling up between them as they had the radio tucked up close to their ears to keep the volume down so it wouldn't wake up the rest of the house. You might think I remember this because I was obsessed with cricket and would go on to play as a pro. But I actually remember it because of the feelings of love, family and warmth. It was easy for me to pretend I wanted to listen to cricket so I could tuck in between them both. I was asleep before I even knew who was batting or bowling.

At the time, I had no idea that in Australia the government had strict rules on who could and could not enter their country. And the colour of your skin was a deciding factor. In those days, Australia did not like to let Black people come to live in their country. It was different, though, if you were a sportsperson. Then the rules didn't really apply.

West Indies cricket teams and Jamaican sports teams, along with track and field athletes, had enjoyed sporting equality for some years – the chance for Black people to go up against others as equal competitors. Anyway, while I was dozing, I'm sure my mum and dad must have felt been really happy about that, thinking back.

So, in 1975 (a long time ago!), when I became one of those Black players competing on equal terms and playing in Australia, I'm sure my parents had thoughts and feelings beyond family pride. My dad was in the stands watching me play my first match for West Indies against Australia in Brisbane. My mum was listening to the broadcast on the radio in bed.

What me and my family had in that moment was a form of equality. And I had that throughout my sporting career. As I have become older and wiser, I feel a mixture of emotions about that.

I was really lucky that in my chosen career as a fast bowler, I was not discriminated against because I was Black. I was, most of the time, accepted. There is some guilt because it was so easy for me when the vast majority of Black people couldn't have imagined such a situation . . . and that it took me a while to realize it.

WE ARE AS GOOD

I didn't know for a long time in my life how important it was to be 'seen' by other Black people. To say, 'Hey, here we are taking them on. We're as good as them at anything. Not just sport.' In some parts of the world, Black people have never seen other Black people do that. In South Africa, for example, when Black people didn't have the same rights as white people, they weren't able to watch the great West Indies cricket team beating everybody else. Why? Because the country did not want Black Africans to see other Black people triumph, showing how good they themselves could be. They didn't want people to start getting ideas in their heads.

What we have described so far in this book amounts to something called *systemic racism*. This means that every part of life is organized to keep the Black person down and the white person on top. But sport is different. It hasn't always been that way, but I want to highlight it now as we're talking about equality.

Black people have tried really hard to get equality. They gave their lives fighting for the Americans and the British in the belief that, once the guns and bombs and death had stopped, they would be seen in a new way. But you won't have read about those stories because it is another part of history that has been ignored. Black people fighting in wars – to be recognized and treated as equals – has been covered up like it's a dirty secret.

THE ULTIMATE SACRIFICE

In America at the start of the First World War, Black people were not allowed to vote. But as soon as the fighting forces realized they didn't have enough men, Black people could die for their country. It is worth repeating. They weren't allowed to vote. But they were allowed to die in a war.

From 1916, many Black soldiers joined a group called the 369th Infantry Regiment. They were an all-Black unit and had a nickname, the Black Rattlers. Sadly, many white American soldiers said they didn't want to fight with the Black Rattlers. So the army decided that the Black Rattlers would fight with the French army instead. The French were happy to have them. The Americans were angry that the French soldiers wouldn't treat the Black soldiers badly, and got more and more worried when they saw them treating them, well, like normal and equal human beings.

Some American generals, like General Joseph

Pershing, wrote terrible things about Black soldiers. Pershing wrote a booklet on how they should be treated. Here are some of the things he said:

- The Black man is inferior to the white man
- The Black man is a menace to the American
- They are unreliable
- Don't eat with them or shake their hands
- Don't praise them.

During the First World War, the Germans noticed how the Americans were treating their Black soldiers and they produced booklets of their own that said that Black people should stop fighting for a country which hated them and that 'the Germans have never harmed you'. They dropped these booklets on the soldiers from aircraft.

The Black Rattlers proved General Pershing and white soldiers wrong. Anyone would have thought they were more concerned with shaming and embarrassing Black soldiers than winning the war.

It certainly didn't sound like they were fighting for the same side at times. The Black Rattlers fought bravely and brilliantly in many battles and earned another nickname: the Harlem Hellfighters. They were in the trenches under attack for 191 days – longer than any other American fighting unit. They never lost a single piece of ground. They suffered fifteen hundred casualties – more than any other American regiment. And they were the first fighting unit to make their way to the Rhine River in Germany, which was an important place to control during the war.

ACCEPTED AT LAST?

After the war was over, it seemed, for a short time, that Americans were proud of the Black Rattlers and all the other Black people that fought. In front of as many as 5 million people, the Black Rattlers marched through New York City to Harlem in a victory parade. It was February 1919. The newspaper the *New-York Tribune* wrote that white Americans had never welcomed their Black countrymen with such love before. The *New York Times* said that, to those there, the Black soldiers 'appeared seven feet tall'.

So, were Black Americans finally accepted? They had proved they were as brave, as strong and as smart as white people. They had fought and died and been wounded for the same cause. This was equality, right? Of course not. The US military was so afraid that Black people might be considered as equal, they had to do something about it.

BANNED

General Pershing, the same man we met above who had called Black people 'a menace' and said that no one should shake hands with them, led another war victory parade through the streets of New York. To wild and deafening cheers, more than 25,000 soldiers marched behind him. The Black Rattlers, though, were banned from taking part. The Americans also stopped the French from including the dead Black Rattlers in a war memorial, and Black soldiers were banned from victory parades in Paris, too.

Around 400,000 Black Americans fought in the First World War. There were more than 2 million from countries in Africa and South-east Asia, and 1.5 million from British India. Overall, there were around 4 million non-white soldiers in the First World War fighting on the same side as the Americans and British. All of them were banned from the victory parades. All of them. I was taught at school that the First World War was won by white people. It looks as though that wasn't true, right?

There are two thoughts as to why the Americans and British did not want non-white fighters in the parade. One made more sense than the other.

The first was that lots of people firmly believed that white people were better than Black people. And if they then saw that Black people could be just as good at fighting, being brave and winning battles, then white people would not look so superior.

The second was that if Black people saw that

people like them could be just as good at fighting, being brave and winning battles, then they might think they could take control. Crazy, huh?

So, the heroic stories of Black people were kept out of the war history books. And it wasn't only history books about war that ignored what Black people had done.

DID YOU KNOW?

Just like the Black American soldiers, people of colour across the British Empire believed it was their duty to fight in the First World War to show them they were just as good. The British War Office did not want them, though. But people from the West Indies were determined to fight anyway. So many, in fact, that a special fighting unit was made. It was called the British West Indies Regiment (BWIR).

Soldiers of the BWIR received lower pay than the white solders. And at the start, they were given back-breaking jobs like digging trenches, stocking weapons, cleaning toilets or laying telephone wires, which was very dangerous. In total, more than 15,000 served. 185 were killed in action, and more than one thousand died from illness. They fought in the Middle East, France and Flanders.

Soldiers of the BWIR had to deal with a lot of discrimination, from white soldiers and also from the authorities. When they were denied a pay rise that was given to the white soldiers, it was the final straw. A mutiny broke out and lasted for four days. How did the British react? Sixty of the BWIR were sent to prison and one was shot by a firing squad . . .

BECAUSE OF THE FORGOTTEN

Who can forget those days stuck at home during the COVID-19 pandemic? We couldn't go out. We couldn't see friends or family. It was a really difficult time. And then they invented a vaccine which worked. That was a great day for celebration. Normal life would soon return.

Let's think for a second about the amazing scientists who made that possible. Heroes and heroines, one and all. We owe them so much. They saved our lives, if you think about it. This is, of course, what scientists do. And they have been doing it for years. The history of medicine is a list of wonderfully brilliant finds by brilliant minds.

But what about the very first person to discover vaccines in the western world? Let's think about that brilliant mind. Think of the gift of life that they gave to the world. Think of the way they were cheered and remembered. Think of the pride their friends and family felt.

In 1721, a disease called smallpox was out of control in Boston, USA. The disease killed three people in every ten who caught it. The slave traders, who had introduced the illness in the mid-1600s, were not as badly affected because smallpox had been around in Europe for a long time.

The only hope of keeping as many people as possible safe was to put those who arrived on the ships into Boston in quarantine, a bit like in COVID-19. Those who could left Boston. But most people couldn't afford to leave, so they stayed, frightened. Until someone very special came along . . .

ONESIMUS

That was until a man called Onesimus said he had a way to treat smallpox. The problem was, Onesimus was a slave from Africa. He had told his owner that he had been protected against smallpox in Africa. What Onesimus described was called *inoculation*. It doesn't sound like a very nice process, but here goes: a small amount of pus (eugggh!) was taken from a person infected with smallpox and rubbed into a cut on the arm of someone who didn't have smallpox. This caused their body's immune system to start fighting the small amount of the disease. In a lot of cases, this meant that their bodies were able to fight off smallpox each time they came into contact with it.

The other slaves who were with Onesimus said they'd had the same treatment and believed they wouldn't get sick. Onesimus's owner, Cotton Mather, had a real job on his hands to convince the other slave owners and powerful white people in Boston that a slave, of all people, had the answer to their problems. As it turned out, those people hated Mather for telling them that Onesimus had found a way to stop people getting sick. *How could a slave possibly be right?* they said. Mather was so unpopular that a bomb was thrown through the window of his house.

Eventually, doctors realized Mather was right, and Onesimus's method started to save lives. Towards the end of the eighteenth century, a vaccination was developed against smallpox thanks to Onesimus's inoculation method. But

Edward Jenner, an English physician, got the credit and was hailed as a pioneer. He was white.

As for Onesimus, no one knows what happened to him. Some historians say he was able to buy his freedom from Cotton Mather. Let's think about that. The man who helped beat smallpox in Boston and saved so many lives wasn't even given freedom. He had to buy it. And, years later, a white man took the credit. To this day, smallpox is the only human disease that has been completely eradicated (which means it doesn't exist any more!)

White people and slave owners just couldn't imagine the idea that a Black person was capable of such brilliance. And, in the hundreds of years since, the brilliant things Black people have done continue to be ignored or kept out of the history books. Onesimus was an unlucky trendsetter as well as being important in saving millions of lives.

LEWIS HOWARD LATIMER

Here's another example of someone overlooked for their achievements because of the colour of his skin: Lewis Howard Latimer. Who was he? A genius, simply put. But one you will probably not have heard of because he was a Black man.

One of the first inventors you might find out about at school is the inventor of the lightbulb. Who do you think that is? Most people would say it was Thomas Edison. That's what everyone thinks! But, actually, he didn't invent a lightbulb that really worked.

Thomas Edison made a lightbulb, for sure. But it had a problem. It used a piece of paper (called a carbon filament) that burned out super fast – so fast, you could snap your fingers and it would go out! The person who made a lightbulb that could actually be useful was a man named Lewis Howard Latimer. Around 1880, he invented a longer-lasting carbon filament. This made the lightbulb last for years. And then he designed a way to mass-produce these longer-lasting lightbulbs so that many people could benefit from them. Latimer even helped set up streetlights in cities like New York and London!

So, Edison did invent the first lightbulb, but it didn't work well. Latimer's invention made the lightbulb actually useful.

Another cool thing about Latimer is that he helped with the invention of the telephone! He made the drawings for Alexander Graham Bell's idea. But people don't talk about that much either.

GARRETT MORGAN

There are other Black inventors, too, who did amazing things but aren't talked about enough. For example, Garrett Morgan, who invented the three-position traffic light. You know, the red, yellow and green lights you see on almost every street? He also made a special gas mask that saved people's lives. But, again, most people don't know his name.

Morgan travelled all over America selling his gas

mask, but he realized fire departments wouldn't buy it if they knew he was Black. So he had to hire a white actor to pretend to be the inventor. Some people say his masks were even used by soldiers during the First World War. I wonder how many lives they saved?

OTIS BOYKIN

Heard of this name before? Nope, didn't think so. Otis Boykin was born in Dallas, Texas in 1920. He invented a wire precision resistor. Now, I'm not entirely sure exactly what it does, but I do know that radios and televisions wouldn't work without them. His greatest achievement was inventing the control unit for the pacemaker. A pacemaker is a small medical device which is fitted inside the hearts of people who are unwell with heart problems. How many lives has *that* saved?

DID YOU KNOW?

Black minds are brilliant, aren't they? You could write an entire book about Black inventors and their inventions. Here's a few more: Edmond Berger invented the spark plug (your family car wouldn't run without it!); Elijah McCoy invented the automatic engine lubricator to stop a train engine getting too hot; George Washington Carver came up with clever ways to farm, like crop rotation and looking after the soil, which helped former slaves in Alabama; Alexander Miles invented automatic elevator doors; Thomas J. Marshall, the fire extinguisher sprinkler system; Lyda D. Newman, a hairbrush; W. A. Martin, the modern door lock (stops people getting into your house); William B. Purvis, an improved version of the fountain pen; Marie Van Brittan Brown, the first closed-circuit home security system (also stops people getting into your home!); J. A. Burr, the modern lawnmower; Frederick McKinley Jones, a portable air-conditioning unit (keeps you cool); Dr Shirley Ann Jackson, the technology behind the fax machine and fibre-optic cables; and Patricia Bath, a laser tool for eye operations.

MATTHEW HENSON

Until very recently, if you typed into Google: 'Who discovered the North Pole?' the answer would have come back as Robert Peary. In fact, there is now a big chunk of evidence that it was actually a Black man called Matthew Henson.

Henson, who was born in 1866, three years after slavery ended in America, was Peary's teammate. They shared the dream of being the first humans to stand on top of the world. For twenty-two years, they went on journeys all over the world. Seven times they tried to conquer the pole.

Their adventures in the Arctic began in 1891, and together they were able to draw a map of the Greenland Ice Sheet. Yet they kept failing to be the first to Earth's northern-most point.

Their eighth and final try to make it to the North Pole came in 1909. Henson believed that learning the language of people who lived in the area could make the difference. He was the only member of the team to do so.

In freezing temperatures, cutting winds and a mist that blocked out the sun, finding their way was hard. When the fog cleared, Peary and Henson realized that they had walked past the North Pole! It meant that Henson, who had been in the front sledge, had been the first man to arrive. Henson said: 'I could see that my footprints were the first at the spot.' Henson had made history.

There would be no victory, however, for Henson. Peary was really angry that Henson had got there first and barely spoke to him again. 'It nearly broke my heart,' Henson said.

On their return, society treated the pair very differently. Peary was given one of the best jobs in the US Navy and travelled the world as a superstar. Henson took an office job in New York and later parked cars for a living. It took 28 years for Henson's achievements to be recognized.

DID YOU KNOW?

Without Black people, we would not be tapping our feet in the same way. Rock and roll, country music, blues and jazz music were born from the plantation fields back in the slavery days. Music was one of the few things which helped Black people to forget about the horrors of slavery for a bit.

BECAUSE BLACK PEOPLE ARE AS GOOD AS ANYBODY

So these are some stories about the Black people who have done great things and then been ignored or forgotten. You may have noticed that none of them were sportspeople. Black people in sport don't have this same problem. If you win, you are seen. If you are good enough, you play. There can be no doubt about who is fastest, strongest, fittest or most skilled. The finishing tape does not seem to care about the colour of your skin.

Maybe you know this. Maybe you don't. The greatest sports team ever was the West Indies cricket team, the one that I was a part of. No team has been so successful or as unbeatable over such a long a period of time. Ever. This is not a boast; it is a simple fact. Between June 1980 and up to the start of March 1995, West Indies did not lose a series. We beat everybody for fifteen years, both home and away. No other sporting team anywhere in the world was so good for so long.

Is that West Indies team forgotten? No. Books have been written about it, movies made. I know that without being part of that team, I would not have worked in TV. But there is no doubt that when we were winning, there was an effort by some in the cricket world and the media to complain about what we were doing and how we were doing it. And that's because the story of West Indies cricket is one about a mainly Black team taking on and beating 'white supremacy'.

BLACK PEOPLE AND CRICKET

Hundreds of years ago, Blacks were not allowed to play in proper matches. It wasn't until 1906 that a West Indies touring team actually had any Black players! And it wasn't until 1948 that a West Indies team even had a Black captain. A Black man wasn't clever enough, apparently. George Headley was the first Black man to be made captain of West Indies. Every West Indies team from 1900 to 1957 had been captained and managed by a white person.

The teams that Headley was a part of, as well as the ones before and the ones after, were seen as entertainers rather than winners. They could be brilliant one day, and awful the next. West Indies were not winners. This made them extremely popular with fans in Australia and England because it meant that the white people were still at the top of the pile. When the West Indies eventually won their first Test match in England in 1950, it was a huge moment for all West Indians and brought great joy.

PROFILE: SERENA WILLIAMS

Serena Williams is the second-best female tennis player of all time in terms of major trophies won. She won an incredible twenty-three grand slams, just one behind the record. But she's my number one – and many others', too. That's because in the modern sporting world, she has probably done more than anyone to show that Black people are brilliant. And she has used her fame to improve people's lives.

All of those horrible ideas about Black people being lazy, dull and unskilled have been destroyed by her booming, powerful forehand on tennis courts all over the world.

Serena started playing tennis at just four years old in Compton, California. But *playing* probably isn't the right word. She was working. While other kids were off having fun, she was practising, hitting balls for hours on end. It probably helped that her older sister, Venus, was also brilliant at tennis, a sport which was often seen as for white people only. Certainly at the start of her career, Serena and her sister experienced racism. People thought they didn't belong. But between them, they ended up dominating the women's professional game from the 1990s through to the 2010s. You could say they ended up owning women's tennis. Suddenly, tennis was a sport for Blacks, too.

It is hard to put into words what a powerful and inspiring pair they are. Imagine being a young kid growing up in a poor area, which the two girls did, and watching them beat everyone? Loads of people started playing tennis because of them.

Serena is also a hugely successful business-woman. So if hitting rapid serves or drop shots isn't your thing, she shows you that there are other ways to excel.

Serena has also given back. There are far too many examples of the foundations and charities that she has either set up or supported. In fact, to write down the full list in this book would take page after page. She has supported hospitals, schools (even one in my home country, Jamaica), the homeless, the poor, earthquake victims, abuse victims, those who can't afford legal support, and medical charities. She has done this with no pat on the back asked for or expected.

BEATING EVERYONE

My first tour as a West Indies player was to Australia in 1975. And it was a wake-up call. We were abused on and off the field by the fans, who sometimes mentioned the colour of our skin in their insults. We were absolutely smashed by the Australians, losing five of the six games.

I was shocked by how aggressive the Australian team were. They had two terrifying fast bowlers called Dennis Lillee and Jeff Thomson, who bowled so fast that if our batters got hit by the ball, they would be left bruised and in pain. It was part of the game. 'Lillee! Lillee! Lillee! *Kill-kill-kill*,' the crowd would chant.

After losing to Australia, West Indies decided to find some fast bowlers of our own. I was one of them. As I said earlier, my nickname was Whispering Death. This was because when I was running in to bowl, I was very quiet, and the umpire, who always had his back turned to me, of course, could not hear me coming. The *Death* bit? Well, the cricket ball could kill at the speed that I bowled.

We also had a superstar batter. Viv Richards was one of the all-time greats. He was so cool. He would swagger to the wicket with his head held high. He was putting on a show. He was saying: 'If you're going to fight me, I'm gonna fight back.' We were as good as anyone. *Equal*, for that matter.

Viv saw cricket as a way that we could be treated the same as everyone else. Every match, he would wear a sweatband on his wrist of green, gold and red. Green for the colour of the African plains, gold for what was stolen, and red for the blood that was spilled. When Viv was at his most famous, they used to sell those wristbands to kids in English sports shops. I wonder how many mums and dads would have bought them if they'd known what those colours meant?

We were a real team. We felt like we were representing Black people everywhere. Showing that we could be as good as anybody. For some of my teammates, that was a big motivation. Others were trying just to do themselves and their families justice.

And we did that. As I said, we beat everyone. And when we were beating everyone, it sure got interesting. A bunch of Black guys coming together and doing so well had never been seen or heard of before. And the old colonial powers didn't like it. Suddenly they wanted to change the rules of the game to try to stop us, saying that we shouldn't be allowed to bowl so fast. We scared the batters with that small, hard red ball hurtling towards them at more than ninety miles per hour. If it hit you, it really hurt.

Despite the fact that the Australian team gave us the idea to have fast bowlers of our own, other countries didn't like it and were always complaining. When we went back to Australia and gave them a taste of their own medicine, the same crowds that chanted 'Kill!' booed when one of their players got hit. The newspapers, all over the world, loved to stir things up and report all this in a racist way, too.

What these people wanted was a return to the old West Indies teams, the entertainers who would play well one day but not the next. They didn't like us winning so much. They wanted us to lose with a smile and say, 'Thank you for the opportunity.'

No way. Nothing could stop us.

But there were Black sportsmen and sportswomen who came before us, too. I've picked out some who were inspiring and we will meet them below.

PROFILE: FRITZ POLLARD

Fritz Pollard was way ahead of his time. He was an American football player. And not just any player – he was the star player for the NFL champion-winning team in 1920, then became the first Black NFL coach in 1921 and the first Black quarterback in 1923. A Black coach telling white players what to do in America in 1921! It is mind-blowing.

Pollard's story shows what life was like for a Black man in America during that period. He'd actually wanted to be a baseball player. But Blacks were banned from that sport. So he tried American football instead. At university, he was racially abused by his teammates, until they realized he was their best player. His professional career began with Akron Pros in 1919, the year of terrible race riots in America. He was abused by his team's supporters and even other players of colour.

Akron won the first ever national championship, going the entire season without losing. When the team was awarded the trophy, Pollard was not allowed to attend the ceremony. The following year, Pollard was player-coach. There wouldn't be another Black coach in professional American football until 1989. In 1923, he became the first Black quarterback, the most important position, when he played for Hammond Pros. It would be almost fifty years before another Black man played the same role for a team. He died in 1986, aged ninety-two. It took another nineteen years for Pollard to be inducted into the American football Hall of Fame, which remembers the most important players and coaches.

PROFILE: JACK JOHNSON

Jack Johnson was a Black boxer who held the world championship title from 1908 until 1915. But was he loved and celebrated for being so good? No. He caused such anger in America that he had to leave the country. People hated him for being a Black man who was strong and great at his sport. You may have heard the expression 'great white hope'. Well, Jack is the reason that it exists. Many white people in boxing were desperate to find someone of their own skin colour who could beat him. When they couldn't find anyone, Jack was accused of made-up crimes. This was 1913. It wasn't until seventy-two years after he died that it was admitted those crimes were invented and he was declared innocent.

PROFILE: ALTHEA GIBSON

Althea Gibson was an American tennis player and a professional golfer. She made history as a Black athlete for crossing what was called the *colour line* in international tennis. The colour line was another way of describing segregation. Here, this meant Black people couldn't play tennis against, or with, white people.

In 1956, Althea became the first Black woman to win a tennis grand slam when she triumphed in the French Open. The next year she would win Wimbledon and the US National Championships, which was later called the US Open. They were grand slams, too. A grand-slam event in tennis is thought to be the hardest to win, and there are only four (Australian Open, French Open, US Open and Wimbledon).

In the end, Althea would win eleven.

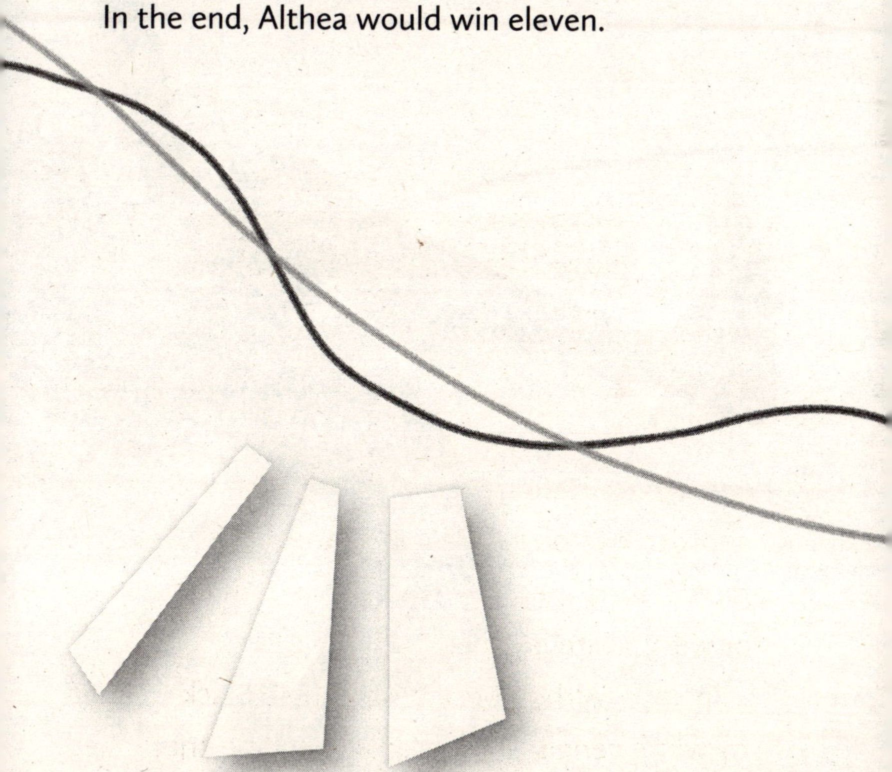

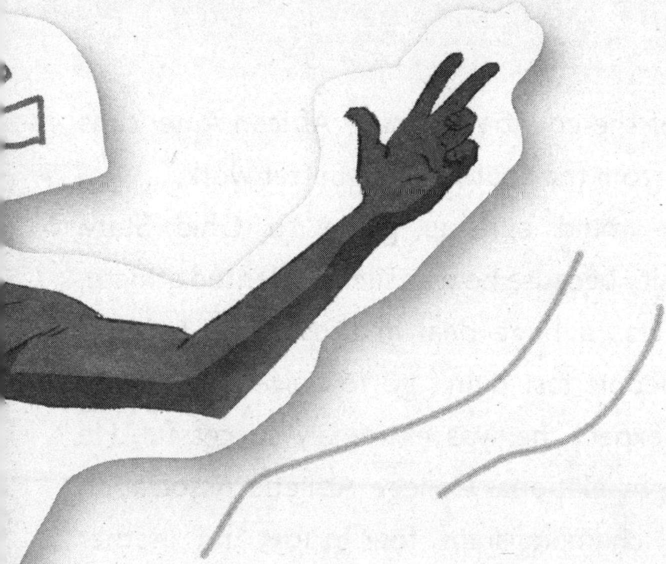

PROFILE: JESSE OWENS

The American Jesse Owens was one of the greatest athletes ever. He did amazing things on the track, winning four Olympic gold medals and breaking several records. But he also did something far more important.

Jesse was born in 1913 in Alabama, a southern state in the USA where slavery had been popular. Jesse's dad was a sharecropper and his grandad, a slave. Jesse later moved to Michigan, a state in the north of the country, as many African Americans moved from the south to find better work.

Jesse would end up going to Ohio State University because he was such a talented athlete, which was a huge deal in those days because Black people just didn't go to university. As you would expect, he was extremely successful. He won eight National College Athletic Association (NCAA) championships, four in 1935 and another four in 1936. But this didn't mean he was treated well. He wasn't allowed to live at the university like the white students, he had to work part time to pay for his education, and when he travelled with the athletics team, he could stay only in hotels for Black people and eat at Black restaurants because of segregation.

On one incredible day in 1933, Jesse broke five world records and tied a sixth in just forty-five minutes! At the Big Ten Championships in Michigan, USA, he set records in the long jump, 220-yard dash and 220-yard hurdles. He equalled the record in the 100-yard dash. He was FAST.

As you would expect, Jesse was going to the Olympics. And there have been few more historic Olympics than the one in 1936 in Berlin, Germany. These games happened at a time when Germany was run by the Nazi Party and Adolf Hitler. This was three years before Hitler started the Second World War. The Nazis believed that the white German people were the best at everything. So you can imagine what they thought of Black people like Jesse.

There was some talk at the time that America shouldn't send a team to the Olympics because of the Nazis. Some people thought the American team should withdraw, while others argued that America shouldn't judge when it also discriminated against minorities. In the end, Jesse and Team USA went, and Jesse would go on to win four Olympic gold medals in Berlin: in the 100 metres, 200 metres, 4 x 100 metre relay and the long jump.

Before one race, a man called Adi Dassler came up to Jesse and asked him to wear some running shoes he had designed. Adi Dassler was the man who founded Adidas. This was the first example of a Black athlete getting a sponsorship deal.

But Jesse had done an incredible thing for the world. He had shown that the Nazis were wrong. Hitler had expected his German athletes to win everything. But they didn't. And the fact that it was Jesse, a Black man, who stopped them made Hitler furious.

On his return to America, there was a parade in honour of Jesse in New York City. But soon life returned to normal. After the parade, for example, there was a party at a hotel. Jesse wasn't allowed to use the main entrance because he was Black.

So I guess you will know the answer to this next question.

Was Jesse properly rewarded by his country for what he did?

No. In fact, they banned him from competing because he wanted to earn money from sponsorship deals. He had to take jobs at a petrol station, as a cleaner and as manager of a dry-cleaning firm. The only racing he did then was for entertainment, against motorbikes, cars and horses.

HOW WE RISE

BY TREATING EVERYONE THE SAME

PROFILE: THIERRY HENRY

Thierry Henry is one of the greatest strikers of all time. He scored 360 goals in league and cup matches, 228 of them for Arsenal, and he became their leading goalscorer. He won the Premier League Golden Boot a record four times, three FA Cups and two Premier League titles. He won the treble with Barcelona. He played for New York in Major League Soccer. Oh, and he also won the World Cup and the European Championship with

France, and was the national team's record goal scorer with fifty-one goals.

Thierry is a good example of a Black athlete getting the respect he deserves. And he is a good starting point for this next part of our story:

We have learned about Why We Kneel.

But here we are going to talk about How We Rise.

We have shown that Black people can be as good as anybody. Now let's look at more examples of being inspired to do exactly what the title of this book says. And that goes for people of all skin colours. If we can ALL be treated fairly, then we can ALL rise together. Everyone's life gets better.

I spoke to Thierry about what it was like to be Black but to be treated with equality, and he told me a story.

'Before I played football,' he said, 'if I walked into a shop with a tracksuit, the security guard is following me. That's the norm. I go with the same tracksuit after I score a hat trick for Arsenal, it's, "Mr Henry, how can I help you?"'

What is the difference? Why do you think that Thierry was not being followed by the security guard any more?

I think – and so does Thierry – that it is because people were not afraid of him. They did not see him as a threat. He wasn't going to steal anything. They recognized him as the striker who scores goals for Arsenal.

Now let's listen to another of his stories. He was in New York City, where he was playing for a local team. He had booked an Uber. He was wearing a tracksuit again, but this time he had a hat on, too. The driver of the Uber pulled up, saw him and sped off.

'In Europe, people know me,' Thierry said, 'and I don't say that in an arrogant way. I am recognizable. I've got a funny face. Big forehead.' He laughs. 'But when I went to America, whoosh . . . I am not known. I was just a Black guy. My colour came back to me. I was reminded.'

Thierry didn't tell me these stories to complain that people didn't know who he was. He was making the important point that to be treated like a normal human being, he had to become famous.

BEFORE FAME

At the start of his football career, Thierry, of course, was not famous. He remembers playing in youth matches in France where most of his teammates were people of colour. And when they went to away matches, they would be abused because of their colour.

He quickly realized football was a way out. Thierry's story, and the story of the French football team, is one about becoming accepted. When France won the World Cup in 1998, there was a lot of talk in France about the number of Black players in the team, some of it negative. When they won the World Cup again in 2018, it was normal to have Black players. That win has helped to change the story about Black footballers. France as a country rose together. Everyone benefitted. You see, it really works if everyone is treated fairly. And having the best football team is a very easy way for people to understand that we are all equal, because your team, your country, your fellow people are waving the World Cup trophy around.

But it hasn't changed the story for Black football managers. When I was writing this, there were only two Black managers in the ninety-two clubs in the English leagues. Here's some more statistics: of the Black players who have played for England for ten games or more, 25 per cent became managers. Of the non-Black players who have played for England for ten games or more, 46 per cent became managers. This tells me that it is okay for Black people to be physical and strong and fast. But, hey, you don't have the brains for the 'important' jobs.

Thierry has been a coach for Monaco, a team in France, Montreal Impact in Canada, the French Under-21 team and the French Olympic team. He won a silver medal with the Olympic team in the 2024 Games. He won that medal after I spoke with him, but he said to me: 'It is still annoying that we get recognized only for physical attributes, rather than mental ones. You have a lot of the [players] in the 1980s or the 1990s that could have been coaches. They had everything. But they didn't even bother, because they knew they wouldn't get the job.'

I think I know why that is. When you encourage Black people or show that they are doing well, the old, historic argument that *white is best* is defeated. It is very hard for society to change that. A lot of people believe that equality means they lose something. They think equality is like a pie. There are only so many pieces of pie to go round. That is not how it works, though.

I think that if more people are treated in the same way, then it is good for *everybody*. Thierry and his France team are an example of that, as I have said. If your football or sports team wins a big trophy, and they have players of different skin colour, it would make everyone feel good. You would feel part of it because that is what being a supporter or fan is about. You are in it together.

What do you think?

ACCEPTED ON THE PITCH BUT NOT OFF IT

When it comes to football, Black players are usually accepted on the pitch, but not always off it. The crowds cheer for you when you're on the field, but on the street, you can be abused. The newspapers and television have a big role to play here. Look at how Black footballers are treated in the British newspapers. When Marcus Rashford, the Manchester United and England striker, took on his government to get free school meals in the school holidays for poor children during the pandemic, one paper wrote an article about what he was spending his money on, strongly hinting that he was some sort of fraud. Raheem Sterling, also an England player, is another footballer who has made 'news' for supposedly showing off about his money. If a Black footballer buys a home for his mother, he's showing off. But if a white footballer buys a home for his mother, he's a good son.

Thierry thinks that social media – Instagram, for example – can make a big difference. Those spaces allow ordinary people to voice their ideas and views. And then other ordinary people see them, and it helps them form their own opinions.

'I see more and more people from my community on TV,' he says, 'having a voice that people listen to. So I know it's possible. So maybe if you change who is at the top to younger, fresher, community-minded people, maybe it will be different. If you have an open mind and you read well and travel, then you are moving away from what your parents told you. It takes time for people to accept something.'

This is really good advice. As you get older, listen to people, read books, go to different places. Take it all in. Think about what it is like to be other people. And come together regardless of skin colour.

If white people and Black unite to beat this racism, it can be done. The Black Lives Matter demonstrations show us that. If you look back at those protests, you will spot that young white people, brown people, Black people were on the street together, all over the world. Young people globally are recognizing that things aren't right (well, a big chunk of them, anyway), and they want to point these things out. So, one would hope that when these young people grow up and have jobs and roles that can make change, things will slowly but surely get better. You really do have the power.

This is How We Rise, together.

PROGRESS?

As the world becomes a smaller place and more information is freely available, and re-education helps to get rid of the old, brainwashed thoughts, progress is being made.

Some time in the middle of 2020, I saw a story about a person who worked in horse racing who had posted some racist comments on his social media platform. He was banned from the sport. His son then posted on social media that he was glad his dad had been banned because he had wanted to talk with him for years about his attitude to Black people, and now it had given him the chance.

Progress, then? Where are we?

'I'll tell you why we made progress,' Thierry says. 'I think what has happened after what happened to George Floyd is . . . people want to know. Before, it used to be our community that was crying and trying to make people understand, "Hey, it's hard, right? I'm here! Hello, we're suffering!" So people didn't feel our pain. They didn't feel my pain. Because as much as you want [to], if you don't live it, you can't see it. Once you live it, you understand. I saw all the communities caring about our community. That's where I think the progress has been made.'

PROFILE: LEWIS HAMILTON

We have already heard from the fastest person on two legs – Usain Bolt. What about the fastest man on four wheels? Lewis Hamilton, who is British, became the first ever Black world champion in Formula 1 when he won the drivers' title in 2008. For good measure, he has won it six times since. That makes him the joint most successful F1 driver in history, standing shoulder to shoulder with Michael Schumacher. Lewis was also knighted by the Prince of Wales in 2021. So he is Sir Lewis, to you and me.

I should also probably say he was the first Black driver to even compete in F1. He holds the record for most race wins, most pole positions and most podium finishes.

His story is one of strength, belief and hard work.

Lewis started go-karting at the age of eight, and it was really obvious from that young age that he was gifted. He started to win everything. One of the first records he broke was when he won the British Cadet Kart Championships aged ten. To help him progress in his career, Lewis's dad had to work four different jobs at the same time to help pay for his racing because it is such an expensive sport.

It wasn't easy. Lewis was bullied at school. And, of course, he was abused because of the colour of his skin. He was the only Black driver when he was racing go-karts and making his way up the ranks of the sport. Maybe people treated him badly because they knew he was so good and they were jealous. But Lewis hasn't forgotten the pain of the bullying and racism.

That is why he has had a lot to say about racism. He is another person who has used his fame to help break down barriers. Very early on in his career, it was clear he was being treated differently when in five of the first six races, he kept getting into trouble with race officials. 'Maybe it's because I'm Black,' he said.

Lewis has always called out the lack of people of colour in motor racing. In 2018, after eleven years in F1, he said, 'Kids, people, there are so many jobs in this sport in which anybody, no matter your ethnicity or background, can make it and fit in.' Lewis was right. When you watch F1 on TV, you often just see the drivers. But there are hundreds of people working behind the scenes for each of those teams, too.

Lewis made sure that when the Black Lives Matter protests were in full swing after the death of George Floyd, he led the way in F1. In the 2020 season, he took the knee before every race and posted on Instagram to complain about how people in his sport were silent. These are some of the words he wrote:

> “*I see those of you who are staying silent, some of you the biggest of stars. Not a sign from anybody in my industry, which of course is a white-dominated sport. I’m one of the only people of colour there, yet I stand alone . . . I would have thought by now you would see why this happens and say something about it, but you can’t stand alongside us. Just know I know who you are and I see you. The way minorities are treated has to change; how you educate those in your country about equality, racism, classism and that we are all the same. We are not born with racism and hate in our hearts. It is taught by those we look up to.*”

But Lewis is more than a man of words. He is a man of action. He spent millions of his own money to support the cause. He set up the Hamilton Commission to find ways in which motorsport can get young Black people interested in science, technology, maths and engineering. He then set up Mission 44 to help young people from poorer backgrounds to be educated properly and find good jobs. On top of this, he has supported animal rights, environmental causes and human rights projects. It is a wonder he finds time to be the fastest man on four wheels. Lewis was named as one of the most influential people in the world in 2020.

PROFILE: MAKHAYA NTINI

Change does not happen overnight. There is no magic wand. No quick fix. Change happens over many, many years. And I think we have shown that in this story so far. Black athletes now usually get the respect they deserve. In the past, they didn't even get the chance to show what they could do.

But the question no athlete wants to be asked – Black or white – is whether they feel like they have done so well because rules have been made specifically to help them succeed. If they think they might have been picked for a team because of the colour of their skin rather than for the talent they have shown in their chosen sport. This is something called *positive action*.

So I want to introduce you to Makhaya Ntini. Makhaya played 101 Test matches – the hardest and highest form of cricket – for South Africa. He took 390 wickets. Like me, he was a fast bowler. He is retired now and I have worked with him in the commentary box. Only two other South Africans have taken more wickets than Makhaya for South Africa. He is a legend, a true great of the game. He was also the first Black person to represent South Africa in cricket.

But some people say that Makhaya only played for South Africa because he is Black. This was because of something called 'the quota system' in post-apartheid South Africa. Those people could not be more wrong. But I guess I need to explain more.

WHAT WAS POST-APARTHEID SOUTH AFRICA?

In 1994, there was a general election in South Africa, which was won by Nelson Mandela's political party, the African National Congress. It meant that the South African legalized system of Black and white people being kept apart in their workplaces, public transport, restaurants and loads of other areas was over. That system was called *apartheid*. People of all colour were free. Yep, it took until 1994 for Black people to have freedom in South Africa. And we thought it was bad in America where they had to wait until the 1960s!

WHAT WAS THE QUOTA SYSTEM?

To help Black people get equality in post-apartheid South Africa, a rule was made that in sports like cricket, rugby and athletics, there needed to be a minimum number of non-white players. In cricket, there needed to be at least six players in each squad who were non-white. And two of those had to be Black African. South Africa has a lot of Black people, around 75 per cent, so quotas were seen as a fast way to help fix the damage of apartheid.

HELD BACK

Makhaya Ntini is a Black African, and it is true that without apartheid ending in South Africa, he would never have been a professional sportsman. But he is not a fan of the quota system. Makhaya says that players should be picked if they are good enough to play, not because of the colour of their skin. And he feels very strongly about that because after all those matches for South Africa and all of those wickets, what do people say to him? 'That I started because of the quota system,' he says.

In rugby, the quota target for the 2019 World Cup – which South Africa won – was half of the starting team. South Africa rugby World Cup-winning captain Siya Kolisi also disagrees with the quota system. Kolisi said that he believed the great Nelson Mandela would have been against it, too. He is probably right. Remember what Martin Luther King said? He said that Black people should not to be judged on the colour of their skin but the content of their character. As Black people, we have to be true to that. We can't have it both ways – complain about unfairness, but then accept it if it suits.

Maybe you're thinking, *Surely you want this for Black people? To inspire others? These are role models.*

But what if that Black person who gets picked purely because of the colour of his or her skin, rather than his or her ability, is shown not to be good enough? Or worse, to be nowhere near good enough?

This doesn't just go for sport. It should be true for every job. If you start filling positions in sport, business, industry or whatever because you need to tick a box based on skin colour or gender, you don't solve a problem – you create one. In fact, you create lots of problems. For a start, that person might not be capable of doing the job and, especially in an area like sport where lots of people are watching, that person could be embarrassed. How is that good for inspiring someone or being a role model? I don't think this helps us to Rise, or to be better all together. It will also encourage the racists, who will feel empowered to say, 'Told you they shouldn't be there.'

Makhaya told me that he heard this sort of thing a lot. 'I think it was at a time when I already had two hundred wickets to my name,' he says. 'And I was still being called a *quota player*. In any other team in the world, I would have been a senior player, a decision-maker. A guy who was a leader.'

In cricket – and in most sports – there are meetings held between the players, management and coaches with the most experience to talk about things like tactics, a bit like when businesses hold board meetings. Makhaya was the equivalent of the boss of a company with all his experience and in being so good at his job. Yet he was not treated with that same level of respect and was not invited to the meetings. But the guy who had played only a handful of games and was white . . .

'He becomes a senior player because he's not Black,' Makhaya says. 'Straight away, he gets called to the senior meetings. That meeting has to be white people only. And if we say something? All of a sudden, we are ungrateful.'

THE BOY FROM THE VILLAGE

Makhaya was born in a small village called Mdingi. He was a cowherder and he spoke fondly about the spirit of people in the village, sharing food, helping one another with their small farms and animals. 'We were all together; it was the greatest time ever.'

At the age of fourteen, he was spotted by cricket talent scouts. Nothing would be the same again; his life changed – and in many ways for the better – but when he was telling me about it, I could tell that he never found that same village spirit in the cricket teams he played for. He was always an outsider.

He was sent to a school which was well known for making professional cricketers where he faced bullying and racism. Because he couldn't speak English or understand what was being said, his classmates thought they could be racist without him knowing. But he knew. And he had a way of getting his own back.

'Being the only Black guy was always gonna be a big issue,' he says. 'But I had one good friend. And he would tell me what was said. So, at the next training session, I would say to the coach, "Give me the ball when that guy comes in to bat – I'll bowl at him." And I bowled fast, at his body and head.'

The racism, he says, stopped after that.

During his international career with South Africa, Makhaya was always known for his skill and fitness. Every morning before the match, he would run to the ground instead of taking the bus with other members of the team. People were amazed by that. *What a professional*, they thought. The truth was sad, though. Makhaya didn't want to take the team bus because he was an outsider and he knew the white players would not sit with him. It was the same in the hotel dining room.

'You get to the breakfast, and you're the first there. Two guys walk in; they sit someplace else. And then the next person walks in; he goes and sits with them. And so on. They forget that you exist until we are on the field. And this became life.'

Is this racism or the quota system? Probably a bit of both. I understand why the quota system was made law, but Makhaya's experience showed that it was not really the right way to go about things. It allowed people to treat him unfairly, saying that he was only there because he was Black. It defeated the point.

'You've got to do it at grassroots level,' he says. 'That's good. Give those people the opportunities. But when it comes to the top level, international, it has to be all on ability.'

In South Africa, there was also a rule that meant companies and businesses had to have a certain number of Blacks on their decision-making board. But this meant that some companies just put Black people on their board, paid them a salary, but didn't have them involved in the business at all.

But I think South Africa is showing the way forward. It has come a long way in a short space of time. And there are always going to be things that don't work out, bumps in the road and challenges. But having spent a lot of time in South Africa post-apartheid, I am hopeful. I don't want to say the country's methods should be copied exactly, but with Black leaders making decisions and laws, and educating the young about Black history right up to the present day, South Africa – and its people – have a chance. And maybe the rest of the world can learn something from that.

'That's my wish,' Makhaya says. 'If it does not start from our schools, it will never work. Treat people equally, it will change right through to sport, schools and everything.'

DID YOU KNOW?

In South Africa, apartheid started in 1948 and ended in 1994. It was a system of racial segregation with its roots in Dutch and British colonialism. In an election in 1948, a party called the National Party won. This was an all-white party. Many in that party were from the same families of those Dutch and British colonizers. Laws were brought in to separate white people from Black. There were 'strict rules' on where Black people could work and live.

How was it decided where you were allowed to live and work? The National Party divided South Africans into one of four groups based on what they looked like, where they were from, and how much money they had. Between 1960 and 1983, 3.5 million Black people were thrown out of their homes and off their farming land. It caused lots of poverty among Black people and at the same time made the white people richer. In time, 80 per cent of the land would be owned by whites (because the National Party made it law), and non-whites had to carry special papers allowing them to go into restricted areas.

By 1960, Black protestors were being killed in great numbers by police. In Sharpeville, a Black community, police fired on a group of unarmed Black people who were protesting against the government. At least sixty-nine were killed and more than 180 were wounded. I remember hearing about Sharpeville when I was six years old. As I got a bit older and noticed the grown-up members of my family, and in particular my mother, paying attention to events in South Africa, I began to also take notice of the pictures on TV: police officers with scary-looking dogs, shooting unarmed Black folk made an impact. Looking back, I guess that must have been one of the first moments in my life when I realized that something wasn't right with the world.

BY SPEAKING THE TRUTH

Sport had an important role to play in making the world notice what was happening in South Africa. It was sporting organizations which forced governments to do something about it because, and this will not surprise you, South Africa banned non-white players from taking part in all sport. Football's world governing body, FIFA, suspended the South African football federation in 1961, the country was banned by the International Olympic Committee in 1970, and the International Cricket Council did the same – South Africa were barred from the first two World Cups in 1987 and 1991.

Sports organizations saying, 'We're not playing against you because you are racist' was important because, until then, the American and British governments had supported apartheid.

Cricket in particular had an interesting role to

play. The South African government tried to show that apartheid wasn't a problem by hosting cricket tours to their country. They wanted their sports-mad people to watch high-level competition. They were called 'rebel' tours because it was seen as wrong that players from other parts of the world would go to South Africa and play. They were so controversial that they were kept secret, and the South African people were only told about them when the rebel players would land at the airport.

An England cricket team was the first to tour in 1981/82, followed by another tour in 1989/90. Two Australian teams went, in 1985/86 and 1986/87. There was a huge uproar about it. The English players, it turned out, had been paid lots of money to go and basically say that there was nothing wrong with apartheid. A player who agreed to go on such a tour had to be either very ignorant or completely indifferent to what was happening to Black people under apartheid. The phrase 'selling your soul' comes to mind.

You might have thought that taking the money

would have damaged those people's reputations. Well, they were banned from playing for their countries for three years. But once those three years were over, their actions were largely forgotten about. It is a sign of progress that if something similar happened today, those people who took the money would not be so easily let off the hook for what they did.

Still, that was not the most shocking aspect of the rebel tours. Would you believe that two West Indies teams took the money, too? I still can't believe it. They included people who I had thought of as friends and teammates. You can see why a white English player would just be thinking how much money could be made, but a West Indian? It amazes me that Black people, whose ancestors had suffered in the same way that the South African people were suffering, took that money. And some of them did it twice. There were tours in 1982/83 and 1983/84.

At the time, I was angry and felt betrayed. I made my feelings known to those players I knew who decided to put greed ahead of their culture and people.

Was I asked to go? Yes. I was in Australia playing cricket before the second tour and a friend of mine in the team called me to ask if I would be interested. He probably thought he was helping me. I had a knee injury, my career was almost over and he probably thought that I could do with the money. I tried to explain why I wouldn't do it, that the apartheid regime was wrong and I couldn't support anybody or anything that treated Black people in that way. In my opinion, going on a rebel tour was like saying, 'What South Africa is doing is fine.'

The West Indies players returned to their homelands in the Caribbean to find they were hated. People at home thought, *How could they?* A lot of the players who had gone on rebel tours couldn't earn money or find jobs back home. They became poor and lived horrible lives. Some died very young. It's a terribly sad story.

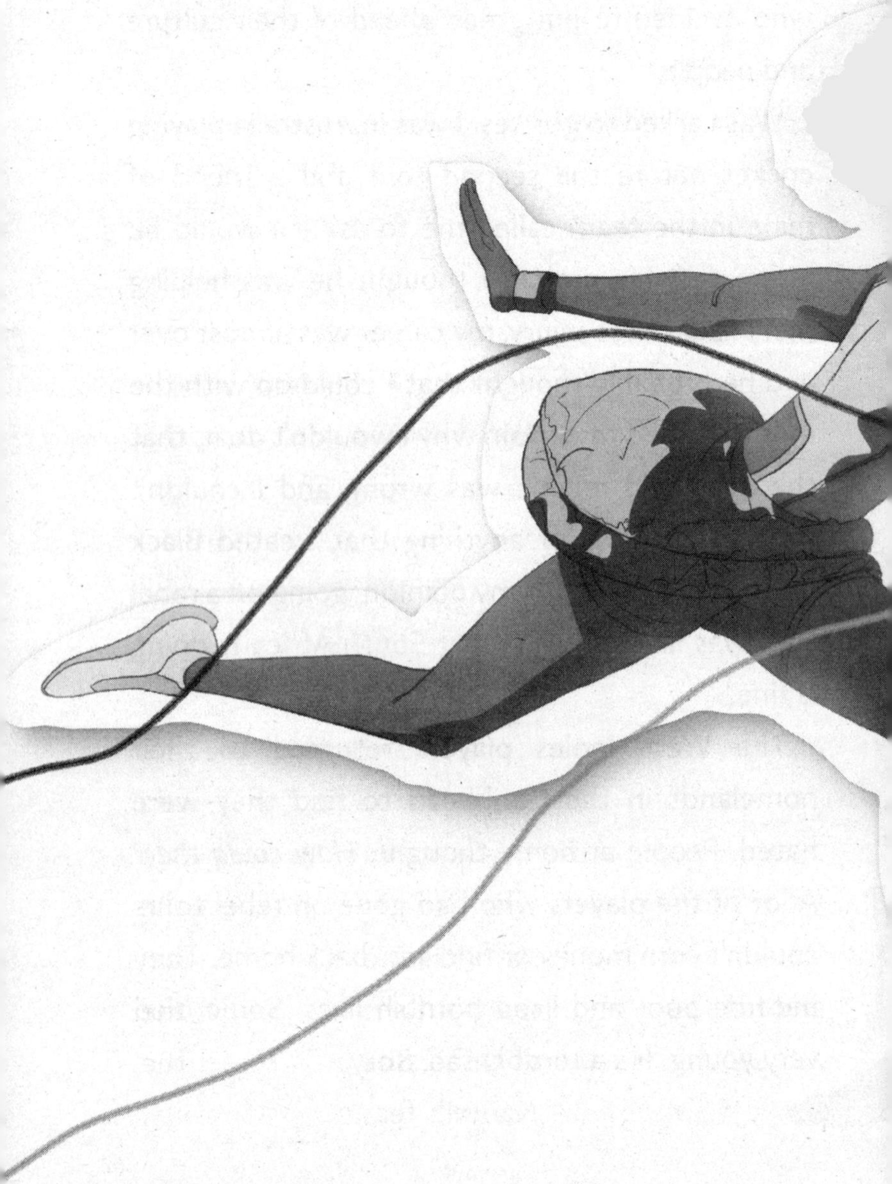

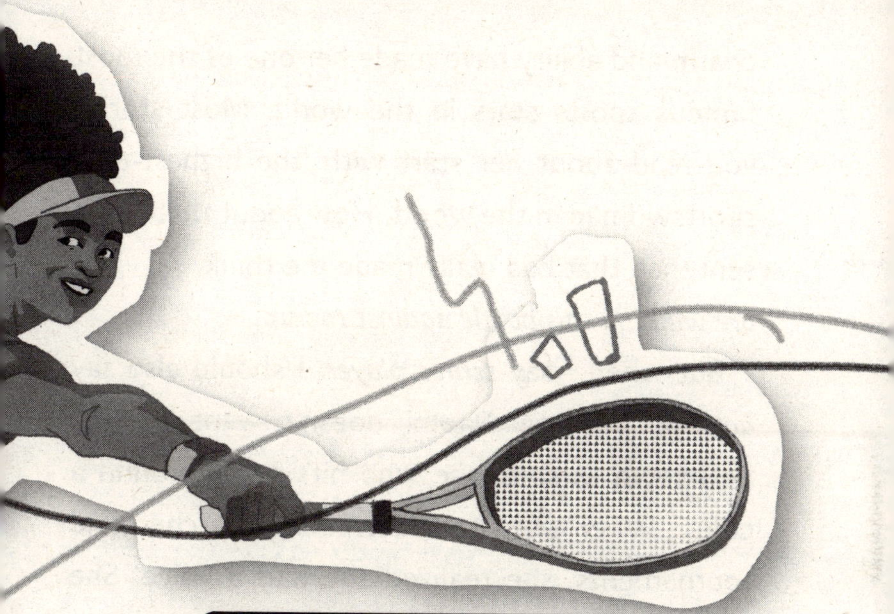

PROFILE: NAOMI OSAKA

There are many figures that Black people can draw inspiration from, both historical and modern day. One such person is Naomi Osaka. Naomi is a professional tennis player who has won two US Open and two Australian Open titles (at the time of writing this book!) Her dad is from Haiti and her mum from Japan, but she has lived in the USA since she was three. She plays under the Japanese flag. Naomi's fearless personality, charm and ability have made her one of the most famous sports stars in the world. Most stories you read about her start with 'the highest-paid sportswoman in the world'. How about that? It's a sentence that has really made me think, *Yes – we are winning this battle against racism.*

But when I say *tennis player*, I should also say *activist*, because Naomi doesn't want to just be known as someone who hits a ball around a court. When she started winning matches and tournaments, she realized she had a voice. She had some power. And she thought, *If I wasn't a tennis player, what would I do to change the world?* It's a good question to ask yourself now and again: *What can I do to change the world?* Because I think you can do anything you put your mind to.

In August 2020, Naomi refused to play a semi-final match in a tournament in New York City as an act of protest after Jacob Blake, a Black man, had been shot seven times in the back by a police officer. I know what you're thinking: *Not another one!* Yes. I'm afraid so. This was just three months after the murder of George Floyd, who we started our story with. Blake survived, but was left paralysed from the waist down. And yet he was still handcuffed to his hospital bed. The tournament organizers agreed to delay the competition out of respect.

Naomi has continued to stand up and speak out, which is not easy. She agreed to have a chat with me about the issues that Black people face in America after she had won her second US Open at the age of twenty-two. I know that I couldn't – and didn't – have the bravery to speak up when I was that age. For her, though, it seemed easy. Her attitude was 'let the haters hate'.

'When I got involved,' Naomi says, 'did I consider there could be a backlash? From fans? Sponsors? I've been asked that question a lot, and I can honestly say it was never something that entered my head.'

And there has been backlash, of course. A young Black woman speaking her mind and showing strength? She was told to 'stick to sports'.

After George Floyd was killed, Naomi joined protest marches. It was the first time she had ever been to something like this. When she posted about the march on social media, she was criticized. To help raise awareness of the BLM movement, she was on the front cover of *Vogue*. She also wrote an article for *Esquire* magazine, which provoked more racist outrage.

'I'm vocal because I believe in the movement and want to try to use my platform to facilitate change,' Naomi explains. 'Being silent is never the answer. Everyone should have a voice and use it. What I'm searching for is equality. For Black people to have the same chances and opportunities as everyone else. I feel my role is to use my platform to shine a light on what's happening so that those in positions of leadership can start working on solutions. Black people have been fighting this alone for so many years, and progress has been slow. Being "not racist" is not enough. We have to be anti-racist.'

What Naomi means is we have to call racism out

when we see it or hear it. Or encourage others to educate themselves about what has happened to Black people throughout history.

The number of Black people shot by the police for no reason in America is very big. So big, that whenever people like Naomi or myself read about another death, we – just like lots of Black people – think, *That could have been me*. For Naomi, the first death that she felt personally was that of seventeen-year-old Trayvon Martin, killed in Sanford, Florida in February 2012.

Trayvon had been walking home after buying food from a shop. George Zimmerman, a local man, saw him and called the police because he thought Trayvon looked suspicious. Then Zimmerman shot and killed him. (Now, do you remember we were talking about white privilege earlier? This is an extreme example. If Trayvon had been white, his white privilege would have meant that Zimmerman wouldn't even have noticed him.) Was Zimmerman quickly arrested? Nope. It took six weeks and a national campaign by Trayvon's parents. I wonder how long it would have taken to arrest a Black guy who'd shot someone in the same circumstances? Zimmerman was found not guilty at trial, arguing that it was 'self defence'.

'I remember when Trayvon Martin was shot and thinking, *Wow, that could easily have been me*,' Naomi says. 'That was a landmark moment in my life and really opened my eyes.' She was fourteen at the time and only lived about a three hours' drive from where Trayvon was shot. 'To see the same things happening over and over still is sad. Things have to change. [But] how do we prevent this movement becoming just another hashtag on a social media platform? It's tough. I don't think Black people can do it alone and we need allies.'

Naomi decided to take things into her own hands. During her 2020 US Open tournament, she came up with a brilliant, powerful and emotional way of raising awareness about the police brutality and hate against Black people in America. In each round of the tournament, she wore a different face mask bearing the name of a victim: Breonna

Taylor, Elijah McClain, Ahmaud Arbery, Trayvon Martin, George Floyd, Philando Castile and Tamir Rice . . . all the way to the final.

Sybrina Fulton, Trayvon's mother, and Marcus Arbery, Ahmaud's father, sent Naomi video messages of support and thanks. These, naturally, gained huge interest on social media, so the message was passed on to a great number of people. 'I'm for ever grateful to the parents of Trayvon and Ahmaud for that,' Naomi says. 'It moved me to tears.'

DID YOU KNOW?

Nelson Mandela was the man who brought apartheid to an end in South Africa. But he had to suffer for it. Nelson was a lawyer and then a politician. He knew that treating Black people differently and unfairly was wrong, so he decided to do something about it. He was highly critical of the government and wanted to have them thrown out of power. He became an influential activist and led his supporters in various acts of defiance. But the government arrested him.

He was imprisoned for eighteen years. His friends and supporters kept the pressure on the government while Mandela was in prison and, slowly but surely, the rest of the world joined the fight to end apartheid and have Mandela released.

When Mandela was freed in 1990, the government had to negotiate the end of apartheid with him. In 1994, an election was held, and for the first time Black people were allowed to vote. Mandela, whose political party was called the African National Congress, was elected president and he served for four years. He was awarded the Nobel Peace Prize. Nelson Mandela died aged 95 in 2013.

STOLEN

This bit of the book might be a little scary. But that's okay because I think it will help you understand what it can be like to be treated badly for having different colour skin. I want you to think about your family for a moment. Or your friends. Apart from when you're being told off for not doing your homework, or when you're falling out with a friend over something, most of the time you are probably laughing, watching TV, having fun, playing sports, trying new hobbies, eating together or going to new places. Maybe you just love watching TV with your mum or dad or brothers and sisters. Thinking of your family probably gives you a warm, fuzzy feeling. Even as an old man, when I think of my parents in this way, I feel the same. Family time is special.

Now imagine that a group pf people wants you to stop having that family time. And they want to take you away from your family and make you live with another family. They don't look like you; they don't have the same way of doing things; they don't speak your language. They are completely different. And, no, you can't see your family at weekends. In fact, you're told you can't see them ever again. Horrible to think about, isn't it?

Well, unfortunately this is what happened to people from two distinct ethnic groups who are known as Aboriginal or Torres Strait Islanders in Australia. Aboriginal and Torres Strait Islanders are also known as *indigenous* people. That means they were people born into families who had been raised in the place where they lived: also known as *native*. In short, they were the first people who ever lived in Australia.

The children of the indigenous people of Australia are also sometimes called the Stolen Generation. That is because of what happened to them when they were taken from their families and made to go and live with white Australians. This was part of a government policy called *assimilation*, which is a word that means becoming part of a group, country or society. This happened because the government didn't want indigenous people in Australia, so they thought that if they put children with white families, slowly but surely, the indigenous people, along with their different skin colour, would die out.

There were other laws which indigenous people also had to suffer. For example, the government banned them from living on the land that their people had lived on for centuries. They were also banned from enjoying their own traditions, like dancing.

So the indigenous people of Australia have been treated horribly. Think about it: their children were stolen from them, they were forced to move from their homes and jobs, they were stopped from doing the things that made them who they were. The number of children stolen was in the tens of thousands. This was happening in Australia from the 1910s to the 1970s.

I know – Australia! That really cool country where the people seem so fun and to be always having a great time! Even the sunniest and happiest-looking places can have a dark, shameful history.

ANOTHER LIAR

It gets worse, though. Indigenous people were also killed in their thousands by the white Australians through the nineteenth century and beyond. The history of Australia is not that different from the Americas. You will remember our friend Christopher Columbus who lied and said he discovered the Americas? Well, Australia had its own liar and thief: this time a British sea captain called James Cook. He was said to have 'discovered' Australia, despite the fact that the indigenous people had been living there for, ooh, I don't know, give or take SIXTY THOUSAND YEARS. Yup – that long. They are one of the oldest peoples in the entire world. Just like Columbus, Cook started killing and hurting the indigenous people when he arrived at a place called Botany Bay in 1770. Yes, that's how long the indigenous people have suffered for.

Eighteen years later, another British sea captain turned up. His name was Captain Arthur Phillip and he returned to Botany Bay to set up a penal colony. This is a place where criminals are sent to live and work as part of their punishment because the country of origin doesn't want them any more.

Captain Phillip decided that Botany Bay wasn't suitable for the colony, so he moved his fleet a few miles up the coast. This would become the world-famous city called Sydney. Captain Phillip's fleet of eleven British ships landed at Sydney Cove on 26 January 1788. This is known as Australia Day, which is still celebrated in the country as its sort of national birthday. Many indigenous people call it Invasion Day.

For the next 140 years, the white people killed many indigenous people. The violence they had to go through was truly shocking, and most of it was too horrible to write about in this book. The last recorded incident of mass killing was in 1928.

What has followed in Australia is the sort of racism that we have already discussed: violence, stopping indigenous people owning homes and having jobs, daily abuse. If you think about what the indigenous people of Australia have gone through – and let's remember, they had their children STOLEN from them – it is quite amazing that they are still there, fighting for the right to be seen, heard and treated as equals. This is a good example of a people rising up together to create change.

And that's why I think it is important that their story is told here. And to help tell it, let me introduce you to an Australian sporting legend. His name is Adam Goodes.

A GOODES MAN

It was a bright, perfect Sydney morning just before Christmas. Adam Goodes was talking to me on his phone via Zoom. Adam is one of the most famous sportspeople in Australia. His sport was Australian rules football, which is a sort of mix of rugby and football. He is also an Aboriginal icon. In our video call, he was sitting on the grass, baseball cap and shades on, talking about some sad moments in the history of his family and of Australia, while watching his daughter, Adelaide, toddle around a play park, eating a rice cracker. She came over to say hello occasionally before wandering off again.

Adam sighed. 'To think in three and a bit more years, someone could come into my house and take Adelaide away from me.'

Most parents experience that fear of their child being taken. But for Adam, it feels very real. Not long ago, it happened to his family. His mum, Lisa, was five when she was taken by the Australian government.

'My nana was saying, "Hide the kids, hide the kids,"' Adam said. 'Mum remembers hearing those boots on the floorboards walking towards her. She started crying under the bed and saw this white hand reach underneath the bed and grab her and her sister. They dragged them both out. And Mum's screaming and looking at my nana, saying, "Why aren't you helping me? These people are taking me away." And that was the last time my mum got to see Nana.'

Adam's is a positive story, though he and his family have been on a difficult journey. He did brilliant things as an Australian rules player. He played for a team called Syndey Swans for sixteen years, he twice won the award for the best player of the year and won two team championships. He showed that Aboriginal people can do great things and he inspired his community But Adam may be best known for how he forced Australia to face up to the horrible moments in its history. And he suffered for it, too.

While playing for Sydney Swans in 2013 against a team called Collingwood on a weekend of Australian Football League matches celebrating indigenous people, he heard a voice scream: 'Goodes, you're an ape!' It was a thirteen-year-old girl. Adam pointed her out to security and she was removed. It was the first time in eight years that he had been the target of racist abuse on the field. Adam escaped to the dressing room and broke down in tears. Why? Because he was being compared to a monkey, something non-whites have had to put up with for centuries. It is hurtful and one of the easiest ways to make a person of colour feel like they are worth nothing. The abusive person is basically saying, 'You're just like a stupid animal.'

The girl's mother tried to excuse her daughter's behaviour, saying, 'She's a thirteen-year-old girl, from a small place in the country, who doesn't get out much.' That is probably one of the best ways to describe racism in these pages. As coming from someone who has not been told about the world and has lived a sheltered, closed life.

Adam did not judge the girl and instead reached out to the family. He offered her support and education. Because the words had come from such a young girl, it prompted conversations all over the country: *Why would she think it's okay to use that word?*

The man who was in charge of the Collingwood team was Eddie McGuire. He said sorry to Adam after the match because the girl was a Collingwood supporter. But four nights later, he went on a

Melbourne radio station and compared Adam to King Kong. Suddenly, everything began to change. Why was Adam picking on a girl? Why couldn't he handle a bit of name-calling? The newspapers, TV and radio started to say Adam was a bully. His social media accounts exploded with people calling him an ape again. Adam was being framed as the bad guy.

But Adam didn't back down. He said Australia had a problem with racism.

'MAN UP'

Adam was booed and abused, week in and week out, for the rest of his career. He was a 'jerk', according to some former players. The girl's mother said, 'He should man up and just take it.'

The abuse ended Adam's career early. He felt that he had given racists a chance to be their worst. His last game was in 2015, and he can't even bring himself to watch the sport on TV now.

These days, the media like to report the story

as something which split the country in half. And that's probably true. On one side, you had people who were embarrassed by their nation, so preferred to pretend it was just Adam picking on a teenage girl. On the other, were those who said it was time Australia faced the truth about its systemic racism.

Time away from the sport gave Adam the energy to do something proactive. He could see that racism was alive and healthy, and that lots of people in the country knew nothing about how indigenous people had been treated. They sure weren't taught about the Stolen Generation in school. Did Australians even understand what racism was? It was like he held up a mirror to Australia and forced people to take a look at themselves. What they saw wasn't pretty. Maybe that's what upset so many people.

On our video call, I took the chance to ask Adam: what has changed?

'I talked to indigenous leaders that have been saying this stuff for fifty years. I said, "Man, is anything gonna change?" They stopped me in my tracks and said, "Look what's changed in [our] time. We weren't allowed to get educated; we weren't allowed to vote. We're now seeing our grandchildren get an education, going to university, owning their own businesses, building wealth – don't tell me that nothing's changed. So, be optimistic – be positive – that this is an opportunity now, more so than ever.'"

BY REMEMBERING WE'VE GOT A CHANCE

When I was writing the final words for this book, I thought back to my last few days living in Miami in 2020. There were boxes all around me, and removal men coming and going. I was moving out of my home in America to go to live in the Cayman Islands. There were lots of reasons for the move, but one of the big ones was that I just didn't want to live in America any more. I just didn't feel safe enough as a Black person.

It was the right thing to do. Donald Trump had just lost the presidential election. But he had spread a lot of hate, fear and division during his first term, and as I write, he is back in charge of the country. I find it hard not to think that America is going to be a very, very dangerous place. When he lost in 2020, I really hoped that the world would see that the treatment of people of colour, people who are different, people who have less money was not right.

I really hope Trump being made president again is just one of those bumps in the road that we have to take to get to where we want to go.

In the last five years, I do think that things have got better.

The main positive development is that many people have realized that we need to teach children more history. Stories about Black people who have done great things are being added to lessons all the time. You guys are now learning that although people might look different to you and have different ways of doing things, that is something to be celebrated. This will benefit people of all colours. Black people will realize that they are not just descendants of slavery. We come from some of the earliest and greatest ways of life. We have a history that we can be proud of rather than ashamed of.

White kids are in these same classes, and they're

learning about all these great things that Black people did, too. They're discovering that Black people are as smart, as important and as brilliant as everyone else. In these learning environments, those outdated ideas of white being superior to Black are never given the chance to grow into something ugly.

What would happen if nothing changed in our education system? The kids would continue to leave class having been taught that all Black people ever did was be enslaved.

But if this change happens, everybody wins. The vicious circle that continuously destroys Black lives stops turning. We get educated, we get jobs, we don't live in poverty, we own homes, the number of people in prison goes down, and – guess what – police forces don't need so much money any more and it can used for other things, like healthcare, building roads and railways, improving lives. And round and round we go. But this time, in a good way.

And everybody rises.

People of all colours have got to come together to keep helping each other. Nothing can be achieved unless white people and people of colour are hand-in-hand in this thing together.

I think back to when I was a kid and my mum and I were on a trip to New York City in the 1970s. She was standing at the window of our accommodation and called me over. 'Mikey, come and look at this'. She pointed to a white kid and Black kid playing happily together. No one is born a racist, and those two kids hadn't yet been affected by the world they were about to grow up in. And she said: 'Mikey, we've got a chance.'

BLACK HISTORY TIMELINE

800 bc: Signs of Africans travelling to America.

Circa 1 ad: Jesus Christ is born in Judea. He is not white, as so many people think.

Circa 3 ad: The beginnings of African–Indian trade.

193: Septimius Severus, the Black emperor leads the Roman Empire for eighteen years.

Circa 440: The founding of the Kingdom of Ghana. One of the earliest and most advanced cultures in history.

711: The Moors conquer Spain and Portugal and rule until 1492.

Circa 890: First trade routes established between West and East Africa and Indonesia.

1100: Stone structures are proof of an early civilization in what would become Rhodesia and later Zimbabwe.

1241: Earliest image of a Black person in Britain found in the Domesday Book.

1440-60: Slaves are taken from Africa by the Spanish to Europe.

1492: Christopher Columbus 'discovers' the New World. Two years later, he takes over Jamaica for the Spanish.

1518: First slaves arrive in West Indies.

1562: Admiral John Hawkins leads the first English slave-trading voyage from West Africa.

1619: Slaves arrive in the English colony of Virginia, America.

1623: Britain takes over the island of St Kitts as their control of the Caribbean begins.

1652: The Dutch establish a white colony in South Africa.

1655: The British take control of Jamaica.

1672: King Charles II's Royal African Company takes slaves from Africa to the Americas.

1721: Black slave Onesimus helps to stop smallpox in America by introducing the concept of inoculation.

1781: 132 slaves thrown overboard from the ship *Zong*.

1770: More than 150 years of killing of the indigenous people of Australia begins.

1804: Haiti becomes the first country to free itself from slavery and gains independence.

1807: The British slave trade is banned, but it is not until reparations are paid to slave traders in 1834 that it actually stops.

1849: Harriet Tubman, an escaped enslaved woman, becomes a conductor on the Underground Railroad.

1863: Abraham Lincoln issues the Emancipation Proclamation that declares all slaves should be freed. Two years later, the 13th Amendment ends slavery in America.

1864: George Washington Carver is born. He will invent ways of farming that help former slaves in Alabama work for themselves.

1865: The Jim Crow laws era begins. It lasts until 1965.

1870: Bill Pickett is born. He will become one of the best-known rodeo stars at a time when one in four cowboys is Black.

1872: Thomas Marshall patents a fire extinguisher sprinkler system.

1877: Charles Joseph Bolden is born. He will become one of the very first jazz musicians.

Lynchings become widespread in America.

1882: Lewis Howard Latimer patents a long-lasting lightbulb filament.

1885: Africa is divided up by the European powers at the Berlin Conference. Some borders are decided by the kind of ruler that you might have in your pencil case. King Leopold II of Belgium is given Congo. He will kill up to 10 million Africans.

1887: Alexander Miles invents the automatic elevator door.

1888: Slavery is banned in Brazil.

1889: W. A. Martin patents the modern door lock.

1890: William B. Purvis invents an improved fountain pen design.

1892: Alice Augusta Ball is born. She will be the first woman and first African American to earn a master's degree from the College (now University) of Hawaii.

1898: Lyda D. Newman patents a new, practical hairbrush.

1899: The Boer War begins. The British put more than 100,000 people in prison

camps and tens of thousands die.
J. A. Burr invents the rotary-blade lawnmower.

1906: A West Indies cricket team includes Black players for the first time.

1908: Jack Johnson becomes the first African-American world heavyweight boxing champion.

1909: Matthew Henson discovers the North Pole.

1910: The Australian government begins forcibly removing indigenous children from their families.

1914: The First World War begins. The British West Indies Regiment and the all-Black 369th Infantry Regiment of the New York Army National Guard serve.

1914: Garrett Morgan patents an early gas mask. Later, he invents the three-position traffic light.

1918: Katherine Johnson is born. She will be a mathematician whose brilliance helps the success of US spaceflights.

1919: Race riots in Britain with Black sailors and Black businesses targeted. American footballer Fritz Pollard begins his professional career.

1920: Inventor Otis Boykin is born.

1921: Scores of African Americans die in the Tulsa Race Massacre.

1922: Marie Van Brittan Brown is born. She will invent the first closed-circuit home security system.

1929: Martin Luther King is born.

1936: Jesse Owens wins four gold medals at the Berlin Olympics in front of Adolf Hitler.

1939: The Second World War begins and will last until 1945. Soldiers of colour play a huge role.

1940: Frederick McKinley Jones patents the portable air-conditioning unit.

1942: Muhammad Ali, the Greatest, is born.

1943: Winston Churchill diverts food to British soldiers, causing famine in Bengal, India. Millions die.

1948: Apartheid begins in South Africa. The *Empire Windrush* arrives at Tilbury docks.

1955: The Civil Rights Movement in America begins.

1956: Althea Gibson becomes the first Black woman to win a tennis grand slam at the French Open.

1957: Ghana becomes the first African nation to be independent after colonial rule.

1960: Sixty-nine Black protestors against apartheid are murdered by police in Sharpeville, South Africa.

1962: Jamaica gains independence. The Commonwealth Immigrants Act is passed in Britain to reduce the number of people coming to the UK from former colonies.

1964: Nelson Mandela goes to prison on Robben Island. Martin Luther King delivers his 'I Have a Dream' speech.

America's Civil Rights Act comes into force. Martin Luther King wins the Nobel Peace Prize.

1965: Black people can vote in America. Racial equality activist Malcom X murdered.

1967: Indigenous people of Australia are formally recognized as part of the population.

1968: Martin Luther King is murdered. Enoch Powell delivers his Rivers of Blood speech.

1971: Bernard Coard's book shows how the British school system discriminates against West Indian children.

1973: Dr Shirley Ann Jackson receives her PhD from Massachusetts Institute of Technology. She helps to create technology that powers the touch-tone telephone, the portable fax, caller ID, call waiting, and the fibre-optic cable.

1976: Negro History Week, founded in 1926, is replaced by Black History Month in the USA.

1980: West Indies cricket team beat England 4–0. They will not lose a series for fifteen years.

1981: Brixton race riots.

1982: First English rebel cricket tour to South Africa. Two West Indies teams tour in 1983 and 1984.

1990: Nelson Mandela is released from prison.

1994: Apartheid in South Africa ends. Nelson Mandela is elected president.

1998: Makhaya Ntini becomes the first Black African to play cricket for South Africa. Hope Powell becomes the first Black coach of an English national sporting team. Christopher Alder dies in police custody in England.

2002: Thierry Henry wins the first of two Premier League titles.

2008: Barack Obama is elected the first African-American president of the USA.

2013: Adam Goodes is abused at an Aussie rules match.

2014: *12 Years a Slave* wins three Oscars, including for Best Picture.

2016: Donald Trump is elected president of the USA. Usain Bolt becomes the first sprinter to win the 100 metre and 200 metre gold at three consecutive Olympics. Ibtihaj Muhammad wins a bronze medal at the Olympics. Colin Kaepernick takes a knee for the first time.

2020: Breonna Taylor is murdered, aged twenty-six. Ahmaud Arbery is murdered aged twenty-five. George Floyd is murdered, aged forty-six. Jacob Blake is shot and paralysed, aged twenty-nine. Black Lives Matter protests sweep the world. Joe Biden defeats Donald Trump to become the forty-sixth US president. Naomi Osaka wins a second US Open title.

2021: Kamala Harris becomes US vice president.

2024: Donald Trump is elected US president for a second time.

ABOUT THE AUTHOR

Michael Holding was born in Jamaica in 1954 and played 60 Tests for the West Indies between 1975 and 1987, taking 249 wickets. After retiring from the game, he became a commentator, mainly working for Sky Sports. He is the author of the adult non-fiction title of the same name, which won the William Hill Sports Book of the Year Prize.